Greg Payne
Christmas '71

# MAKE THE TEAM IN BASKETBALL

# MAKE THE TEAM

# IN Basketball

By **CLAIR BEE,** Director of Athletics

New York Military Academy

GROSSET & DUNLAP Publishers New York

*TO*
CLAIR *and* PIC
*my son and my friend*

LIBRARY OF CONGRESS CATALOG CARD NUMBER 61-16640
PRINTED IN THE UNITED STATES OF AMERICA

# Contents

# THE SPORTSMAN'S PRAYER

*"Dear Lord, in the battle that goes on through life,*
*  I ask but a field that is fair,*
*A chance that is equal with all in the strife,*
*  A courage to strive and to dare.*
*And if I should win, let it be by the code,*
*  With my faith and my honor held high,*
*And if I should lose, let me stand by the road,*
*  And cheer as the winners go by.*

*And Lord, may the shouts be ungrudging and clear,*
*  A tribute that comes from the heart,*
*And let me not cherish a snarl or a sneer,*
*  Or play any sniveling part.*
*Let me say, 'There they ride on whom laurels bestowed*
*  Since they played the game better than I.'*
*Let me stand with a smile by the side of the road,*
*  And cheer as the winners go by.*

*So grant me to conquer, if conquer I can,*
*  By proving my worth in the fray,*
*But teach me to lose like a regular man,*
*  And not like a craven, I pray.*
*Let me take off my hat to the warriors who strode*
*  To victory splendid and high,*
*Yes, teach me to stand by the side of the road,*
*  And cheer as the winners go by."*

— AUTHOR UNKNOWN

## MAKE THE TEAM
## IN BASKETBALL

**SKULL PRACTICE**

Plays and teamwork make for perfect performance.

# CHAPTER I

# THE MAKING OF
# AN ATHLETE—YOU!

This book is designed to give the beginner the *right start* in the game of basketball — to aid the "up-and-coming" player in *perfecting his skills* — and to review *the essential parts of the game* for the star.

The dream of every youngster is to "make the team," and basketball is a game any youngster can play. In the last few years the trend has been toward height, but there is plenty of room for *any*-sized player. Height is important, but the advantage is often lost because of lack of speed or poor co-ordination. Speed is also important in today's jet-propulsion game, but it is not imperative. There are thousands upon thousands of players participating in basketball who are of small or medium height and who possess only ordinary speed. These players have substituted spirit; drive; team play; good ball-handling, dribbling, and shooting skills to overcome their opponents' height and speed.

Heavy players of all heights have often found a place on the team because of their rebounding, screening, and "feeding" abilities. Scores of teams throughout the country are sparked by peewees. Most of the good teams I have coached in the high school, college and professional fields had one or more players who could be included in either of these categories.

In a recent survey by the *Athletic Journal,* the hoop game continued to reign as the nation's No. 1 high school and college sport. Basketball teams are fielded by approximately 97 per cent of all high schools and 95 per cent of all colleges. In the high-school category, Texas leads with 1105 teams. Ohio is next with 1065, while Iowa follows with 950. In addition, there are thousands of church, industrial, club and grade-school leagues and teams providing opportunities for players who want to make the team.

How does a good basketball player get his skill? By possessing an intense desire to improve; by starting right; by intelligent and constant practice; by studying the game and its situations; and by developing a spirit of team play, sportsmanship, and self-confidence.

This book provides a down-to-earth, step-by-step approach to the game through the presentation of correct principles and fundamentals. The offensive skills — shooting, passing, dribbling, faking, cutting, screening, footwork, jumping, and following-in — are covered in detail as are the defensive fundamentals covering body balance, floor position, footwork, and guarding the assigned opponent.

The player skills are stressed and profusely illustrated. Offensive and defensive team play, team strategy, and the complex offensive and defensive variations have not been overlooked. It must be kept in mind, however, that this book has been prepared as a sort of personal coach for the player and that reference to the involved offensive and defensive styles of play has been included more for the player's orientation and general knowledge than for practical application.

Can you take it? If you can, you can be an athlete. A good one! Generally speaking, an athlete is a boy or man who is physically fit. He may be big or small, young or old, tall or short, fat or thin — his age, height or weight is not important.

How does a fellow get to be an athlete? By working at it, by being his own trainer and taskmaster. The average youngster today is accustomed to soft and easy living, and the price of being an athlete is high. It takes guts. *Lots of guts!*

Have you got guts? Enough to cut out the snacks between meals and at night before you go to bed? Can you push yourself away from the table when you are still a little bit hungry? Can you stick to the resolution to get nine or more hours sleep *every* night?

## YOUR TRAINING PROGRAM

Not so tough? Well — maybe not. However, there's more to it. You will need a couple of programs — a training program and a practice program. You will want to observe a training program the year around, and if you want to make the team, you will need some sort of a practice program. First, let's take a look at the training program.

### Cleanliness

Shower regularly, starting off with warm water and finishing with cool. Keep your hair cut short and keep it dry (even while showering). Brush your teeth regularly and trim your fingernails frequently. Cleanliness reduces the danger of infection and other illnesses.

### Food

Three meals at regular times each day with a diet which includes milk; meat, fish and eggs (muscle-builders); plenty of vegetables; fruits (vitamins and minerals); salads; lots of water; and a minimum of desserts (candy and pastries). Fats and starches provide energy. Avoid fried and greasy foods, coffee and cold drinks.

### Sleep

The body rebuilds itself during sleep. Sleep affords the maximum in relaxation which is so important for physical fitness. You should have nine or more hours of sleep every night. And, when possible, try to sleep or rest a little before your workouts or games. The more active you are, the more sleep you need. Set a regular hour to go to bed and stick to it — *every* night.

### Conditioning

Try to exercise and do your practicing out of doors. Fresh air and sunshine are great health-builders and increase the ability of your blood to carry oxygen to the cells of your body. While we are on the subject, regularity in all phases of your training and practicing is important. Work regularly and quit when you begin to feel tired.

### Co-ordination

If you lack co-ordination, you have a big handicap. But you can do something about it Shadowboxing, heavy-bag punching, rope skipping, and the use of a medicine ball are fine mediums for the development or improvement of co-ordination. Even a simple game of hopscotch will help. Fencing is excellent, and so is dancing. Seven feet in height, All-American Bob Kurland was awkward during his "growing-up" years. So he decided to do something about it and began to jump rope. Not just during the basketball season but *all year*.

## Feet and Ankles

The good athlete realizes the vital importance of taking care of his feet and ankles and will not take chances on a sprained ankle which may sideline him for several weeks. Make sure that your ankles are taped and that your game shoes are the correct size, light, and roomy enough so that you can wear two pairs of socks. Why two pairs? Because the friction that occurs when you run or stop or change direction will be absorbed by the socks rubbing one against the other, thus lessening the possibility of painful and dangerous blisters. You can help your feet by washing them thoroughly every day and drying them carefully. The application of tincture of benzoin (from your druggist) on your feet for a couple of weeks will help to toughen them.

You are smart enough to realize that a slow and easy warm-up should precede all exercising and practicing, and that trying to play when you are hurt is sure to aggravate the injury if not sideline you permanently.

It's tough. But if you can stick it out after the first big flush of enthusiasm dies, if you can keep going when your muscles begin to complain and ache — and then go ahead and work a little bit more — pretty soon all those lazy, sleepy muscles will awake. You will feel gloriously fit and it won't be work any more — it will be fun! Further, you will begin to think more clearly and react faster and be able to work harder and longer than all those fellows who said it couldn't be done. *And* — you'll be an athlete!

Let's assume now that you are observing all the training rules and are putting yourself through some light exercises to keep your body in condition. That means you are on your way to being an athlete. What is the next step? Well, you want to make the basketball team, so let's think specifically about a practice program. Where do you start? Well, it would be wise to list all the qualities that a good basketball player should have and then try to grade yourself in these so that you will know just what to practice. In Chapter 3 you will find many practice and learning aids to help you improve in certain parts of the game. But first you ought to give yourself this sort of personal analysis, which should include not only basketball skills and fundamentals but the personal and emotional attributes which identify the basketball star.

# RATING CHART

## Personal and Emotional Qualities

| | Excellent | Good | Fair | Poor | | Excellent | Good | Fair | Poor |
|---|---|---|---|---|---|---|---|---|---|
| Aggressiveness | | | | | Mental Reaction | | | | |
| Aptitude | | | | | Patience | | | | |
| Attitude | | | | | Perseverance | | | | |
| Concentration | | | | | Scholarship | | | | |
| Co-operation | | | | | Sportsmanship | | | | |
| Dependability | | | | | Spirit | | | | |
| Desire | | | | | Adherence to Training | | | | |
| Drive | | | | | Team Play | | | | |
| Experience | | | | | Victory Urge | | | | |
| Leadership | | | | | Willingness to Learn | | | | |
| Manners | | | | | Willingness to Pay the Price | | | | |

# CHAPTER II

# ANYONE CAN PLAY BASKETBALL

Yes, anyone can play basketball, and the game itself can be played in a number of ways and in all kinds of situations: one against one; two against two; and on up the ladder. In certain foreign countries, basketball has been played out of doors on a court the size of a football field, with fifty players on each team. You can play the game all alone, too. A game like "twenty-one," shooting from certain spots on the court and keeping score, is great fun even though a player is competing only against himself. Naturally, in developing team play, there is no substitute for playing with others.

## The Little Man

"How tall is he? Can he get through the door without ducking? Yes? Can't he even *dunk* the ball? Huh! Basketball's a tall man's game! What does he think this is — the intramural league?"

Kidding? No, that's exactly how many high-school, college and professional coaches talk when discussing a prospective player. They're *all* looking for the big boys. The expressions "basketball games are won under the boards" and "tall men control the boards" have been broadcast by lecturers and writers so persistently and monotonously that the domination of the sport by tall players has become basketball's Number One menace!

Some years ago, the rules makers legislated the center jump following a field goal out of the game. One of the reasons advanced for this was that the domination of the big man would be lessened. The fallacy was quickly apparent. Held balls and offensive and defensive rebounds immediately increased in importance, and the big man was on his way.

But there *is* a place for the little fellow! He is better co-ordinated, faster, trickier, a better ball-handler, by far the superior dribbler; and his superiority in starts, stops, pivots, changes of direction, and the use of inside and outside screens makes him invaluable in his team's offense.

In the fast break, it is always the little fellow who spearheads the attack. And he's the one who usually comes up with the stolen ball which wins the game! A championship team needs big men but it also needs little men.

### The Little Man's Assets
#### Under 5'8" (Back-Court Play)

You must be a dead shot, an expert dribbler and passer, and a master at handling the ball in the middle position during the fast break. Defensively, you must be a ball hawk and an alert guard and use your quickness and superior co-ordination to protect your under-the-basket defensive play. You will be, in effect, the team's quarterback. So you must be a real

THE LITTLE MAN — THE TALL MAN — anyone can play.

team player, sacrificing your own individual abilities for the sake of the team. You will be called upon to start the plays and supply the setups for teammates and must be expert in this phase of the game. A keen desire to win, a fighting spirit, and mental quickness will help. Go to it, "Fireball!"

## The Average Player

*You're just an average sort of guy!* Well, you've got lots of company, old pal. Just because you are average in height and skill and in coordination and basketball ability doesn't mean you have to be just an average basketball competitor. You can be the versatile one,

[ 15 ]

the player who can play *any* position — back court, high post, low post (yes, little men who work under the basket are often dangerous scorers), or the corner. So, be versatile! Learn to play all the positions.

Defensively, learn to "leech" an opponent on the defense; practice boxing-out (preventing your opponent from getting the ball back after he or one of his teammates take a shot); be a good rebounder — go up high for the ball and bring it down and get it on its way to your basket.

Offensively, develop into an all-around shooter. Too much? Not if you are made of the right stuff. There aren't too many shots to master — lay-in; pivot; turn; hook; one- and two-hand set shots; and the "jumper." That isn't too much of a list. Far from it. Good players know all these shots. Oh, yes — don't forget the *free-throw!* If you're a good shooter from the free-throw line, you can pile up a lot of easy points.

That isn't all; the average player must be a good, hard cutter and know how to set screens for his teammates (they'll love you for it). If you can pass, you can play — on any team. Develop all the passes and make them sharp and fast and right on target. Don't forget your feints with the head and eyes and shoulders and your fakes — with the ball and the feet.

The dribble! Sure — be the best! You can learn this at home — head up, eyes dead-pan and straight ahead, fingertip control, and mastery of the low, high, fast, delayed, and the double-time bounces which make you a dangerous offensive opponent. All this is expected of the average player — get with it!

### THE AVERAGE PLAYER'S ASSETS
#### 5'8" to 6'2" (Back-Court Play)

You must be able to play in the back court or in the corner. Scoring ability is important. If you are the smallest player on your team, you must be able to play like the "little man."

If your team has a little man who takes charge, you must supplement his play by taking the outside lane on the fast break, working into the passing pattern, and supplying the punch by good shooting when it is needed. If your team uses a big man in the pivot, you must be able to get the ball to him or to score consistently should your opponent drop back in front of the man under the basket.

### The All-Around Player
6'2" to 6'4" (Back-Court and Corner Play)

You are what the professional coaches and players call a "corner player," although there have been exceptional players your size who have played in the back court. You must be a hard cutter and a good shot. With your height you will be expected to do your share of the rebounding. In working with a pivot man, you must be able to get the ball to him and cut around him for hand-off plays. Develop a deadly corner shot.

### Heavyweights

Heavyweights? Sure. Plenty of them. Frank Keaney, Rhode Island State's former coach was a big fellow. But his son was bigger. Yes, Warner Keaney weighed 260 pounds! But he played basketball like a speedster of 150 pounds. Pete "Fats" Henry, all-time college and professional football tackle, weighed 250 yet he was a great basketball star. There have been many others.

### The Tall Player

Tall, ungainly "left-footers" have a place in the game, too. Big fellows who sometimes stretch seven feet in height are more or less restricted in their play of other team games, but in basketball they literally "reach" the heights of stardom. Witness such great stars as Bob Kurland, Oklahoma A. & M.'s seven-foot All-American; seven-foot Chuck Share from Bowling Green; Ray Felix of the New York Knickerbockers; Walter Dukes, former great from Seton Hall and the New York Knicker-bockers; Chamberlin, seven-foot, 1/16-inch giant from Kansas University, and so on.

### The Tall Player's Assets
6′4″ to 6′8″ (Corner and Post and Pivot Play)

In high school, college, and with some professional teams you will play center. Therefore you must have pivot and turn shots, a jump-push, and good ability with tap-ins. But — sometime you may have to play the corner. (Note the details for the corner player above.)

## The Exceptionally Tall Player
6′8″ or more (Post and Pivot Play)

The coach will want you under both baskets, so learn to play there. But — make yourself versatile by playing the corner position, too. You must be an expert rebounder and a deadly scorer under the basket. Learn to feed the ball to cutters. Develop your co-ordination by jumping rope, shadow boxing, and dancing. Your height is a valuable asset — use it!

How do you get that way? Not easily. You must practice by the hour, but you must also practice intelligently. This means that you must use the correct techniques.

## What is the Definition of a Good Basketball Player?

Well, he is a fellow who has mastered the offensive skills of shooting, passing, dribbling, jumping, cutting, feinting, pivoting, changing pace, and maneuvering. And he has acquired the defensive "musts" of rebounding and blocking out, and the all-around ability of guarding an opponent.

Is that all? Of course not! The most important part of the definition has been left out entirely. Basketball requires control of the emotions, love of the game, the desire to win, team spirit, understanding of team play, and true sportsmanship.

Good players are born. Nonsense! Intelligent practice and perseverance have been the means to greatness. Hank Luisetti, Stanford University's great All-American player, was generally regarded as the "perfect" player. Was he born that way? No! Hank practiced his shots thousands of times, over and over. Even in the summer months, when his friends thought it was too hot to practice, Hank persevered. He paid the price and he received the reward — one of the greatest players of all time!

*You* can be a great basketball player if you have sufficient self-discipline to persevere and practice. Basketball players are *not* born — they are made — if they are made of the right kind of stuff. *Are you?*

## SO YOU WANT TO BE A STAR

Well, this is a pretty big order, but if you really mean it, you can do it. But you must master *all* the fundamentals of the game to a certain degree and *one* or *two* skills to an exceptional degree.

I am sure you realize that a successful basketball team is one which represents a squad of fundamentalists; that in no other team game is the absence of training in fundamentals so quickly noticed nor so dangerous to a team's success. But I wonder if you realize just how much self-discipline is necessary in the dreary practice of fundamentals; keeping at it when you are discouraged and tired and disgusted. . . . You do! Well, then, that's half the battle, and intelligent practice and perseverance will do the rest.

Every boy is endowed with one or more mental or physical abilities which he can employ effectively in basketball. It is up to each of you to search out and evaluate the particular abilities which you have and then figure out just how they can be applied to your individual play of the game. Perhaps it's the ability to leap high in the air; to dribble a ball at full speed; to "feed" a flying teammate; to maneuver your opponent out of position; to shoot accurately. Or maybe it's the ability to think quickly under fire; to take advantage of a fleeting opportunity and make lightning decisions.

So, after you determine the skills or abilities in which you can excel, you must develop them to a high degree of perfection. But before a fellow can use the basketball abilities and skills in which he is strongest, he has to learn *all* the fundamentals — catching and passing the ball, cutting, screening, dribbling, jumping, guarding, rebounding, and shooting. Then he can determine his strong points and get busy and master the basketball skills they represent until he's expert in their use. That will make him a specialist and he will be on his way to becoming a star.

But we're not through yet. Basketball is played with the head, too. On the mental side, sizing up a situation, spotting a weakness, and then capitalizing on the advantage is just as important as physical action.

Before we go any further, let's figure out just what kind of basketball the tall fellow, the heavyweight, the lightweight, the average player and the shorty must each master to best utilize his physical attributes.

*Now you skyscrapers.* Basketball is the game *you* ordered. You're closer to the basket, and that's where a fellow like you makes his points. Learn the turn, pivot, jump-turn, step-away, tap-in, and the hook shots. Master the fakes and perfect your hand-off ability. And, under the opponent's basket, the tall fellows are the ones who usually come down with the ball!

*Hello, Fat Stuff.* What are you looking so glum about? You're too heavy and too slow? Well, now, that's no *real* handicap. Not if you use your weight and "throw it around" to advantage for rebounds under the defensive boards and use it up in the front court as a post or pivot around which your teammates can cut. You'll have to learn to be an expert feeder, though, and learn how and when to drive for the basket.

*Yes, Skinny, I know.* You think you're too light. But you're pretty fast aren't you? Swell! Be a cutter and a driver. Keep driving and moving all the time. You have the build for it. And — your teammates will think you're tops because you will be making holes and setting up "picks" and blocks for them. You know, Skinny, that's the trouble with most stars; they won't move without the ball. Start right now to master change of direction, stops, starts, pivots, turns, inside and outside screens, and handling the ball while moving at full speed, and you're in.

*Now, Shorty, we come to you.* You can be the spark plug for your team. Yes, by developing into a deceptive passer and learning to be a great offensive and defensive dribbler. You're close to the floor and that's good. Build your skills around that *advantage*. O.K.? Master bounce passes and learn how to keep the ball bouncing on the floor through the use of the dribble just as if you had a string on it. Left hand, right hand, slow time, half time, full time, and double time. Lead the fast break; get that ball and get out in the middle lane when you drive down the floor in a three-on-two situation. *And* get that ball to the teammate who is unguarded under the basket.

# CHAPTER III

# PRACTICE AND LEARNING AIDS

The practice and learning aids presented in this chapter are but a few of the stunts and drills you may use alone or with the aid of one or two friends in getting ready to make the team. Naturally, when you become a member of a team, the coach will prescribe the drills necessary to develop your basketball skills. However, few of these exercises and drills will conflict with those of the coach, and their use in your free time may shorten your learning spell.

You must keep in mind that the best way to learn any game is to *play it*. And it is wise to remember that the right start is necessary, because it is disastrous to practice a skill incorrectly until it becomes a habit. Habits are hard to break! So, when you practice, be sure you are practicing the correct way. Once you develop the habit of executing a skill the right way, you can concentrate on speed, timing, and greater accuracy.

To make sure you are starting right, first ask your coach what techniques he prefers you to use in executing a skill. Second, watch a great player *play* basketball and try to take away with you a mental picture of his execution of the skills. Third, try always to play with and against players who are better players than yourself. You will learn little from playing with or against fellows who are inferior to yourself. In fact, playing with or against such competition may be harmful because the skills that work with or against inferior competition may not work with or against skillful players.

Now take a look at the practice and learning aids, choose those you think will be of help to you — and get busy! The only fellow worse than the quitter is the one who won't start!

## PRACTICE AIDS

### Three-Man Medicine-Ball Drill

The three-man medicine-ball exercise develops the fingers, wrists, arms, back, and stomach and leg muscles. Each player catches the ball and drops back until he rests on his back with the ball fully extended behind him. Then, rising to a sitting position, he brings the ball upward and forward and passes it to his teammate. (Keep the arms extended at full length in catching the ball, carrying it back over the head, and in assuming the upright position). After the three-man exercise has been mastered, the two-man drill may be attempted.

**Two-Man Medicine-Ball Drill**

## Loose-Ball Drill

On a starting signal the two competing players reach for the ball and attempt to secure possession. This drill calls for quick hands, mental alertness, leverage, and strength.

## Developing Quick Hands

Quick hands are a "must" in basketball. Juggling three handballs at one time can be mastered quickly, and you will prove that the "hand is quicker than the eye."

## The Skipping Rope

Rope jumping is a wonderful conditioner and helps to develop footwork. Give it a try!

## Finger-Tip Training

The use of finger tips in passing, shooting, and dribbling insures a light touch, speed, and control. Here the player is using wooden blocks to keep the ball away from the palms of his hands while passing, shooting, and dribbling.

## Spin It!

These three players are spinning the ball on their finger tips to develop "feel" and control. As a player becomes more proficient in this skill, he can transfer the ball from one finger to the other without a stop.

## In the Dark

That's right! Players with imagination develop their passing, shooting, and dribbling skills blindfolded. Try it and see how easy it is to develop touch, control, and accuracy in the dark.

## Shadow Boxing

Sure, boxers use shadow boxing to develop stamina and footwork — but offensive and defensive footwork is also vital in basketball. See if you can hit your shadow.

## Good Hands—Good Basketball

Handballs, tennis balls, grip springs, and expansion bands are excellent devices with which to develop hand and finger grip. Some boys carry a handball in their pocket at all times so that they can practice frequently.

## The Boxer's Stance

A boxer's fighting stance is universally used as the basic basketball defensive position. The only important difference is in the position of the right hand. The boxer's right hand protects his jaw and body, while the basketball player's right hand is used to maintain balance and to discourage passes and the dribble.

## Bag Punching

Punching the light and the heavy bag will improve co-ordination, concentration, footwork, and movement of the hands.

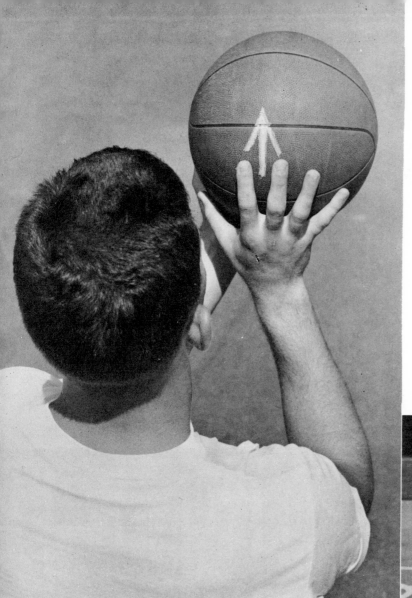

## Tips for Good Shooting

This photo shows the most used position of the shooting hand. The fingers are spread (make a big hand out of a little hand) on the ball, with the fingertips and the thumb (pads) resting *lightly* on the ball (don't grip). The ball is merely resting on the thumb and fingertips. The palm of the shooting hand (right) does not touch the ball at any time.

The left hand is used to help lift the ball to the shooting position. Here, the ball is centered between the first and second fingers of the shooting hand (note arrow). Some players also shoot "off" of the first finger, while many players who possess unusually large hands shoot "off" of the space between the thumb and the forefinger. Note that the ball is carried to the right of the shooter's eyes. When it is carried further up (by pressure from the left hand) it will come back and over the right shoulder and close to the right ear.

Note the position of this player's feet and the flexing of the knees. The knees are flexed so they may be snapped back to provide force to propel the ball toward the basket when making the shot. This knee snap will, of course, be coordinated with the lift and release of the ball by the arms, wrists and fingers. The flexing of the knees will also provide the spring for a leap from the floor should the player be a considerable distance from the basket and need more power to propel the ball.

The weight of the body is carried on the balls of the feet. Some players place their feet on a line, others advance one foot in front of the other (usually right-handed players will advance the right foot and the lefties will advance the left foot). Individual players will automatically place their feet in the position in which they feel most comfortable, and this is fine providing the toes are pointed toward the objective — the basket.

# CHAPTER IV

# OFFENSE FUNDAMENTALS

You are now ready to study and practice the offensive fundamentals. They are easy to learn; the techniques of good shooting, dribbling, and passing accurately are not difficult. Applying them to game play is a different matter. There are many other skills in offensive basketball — feinting; faking; change of pace; change of direction; playing dummy; using teammates for blocking purposes; offensive rebounding; and utilizing stops, rolls, and pivots. Further, there is the matter of moving without the ball — cutting and screening and setting up plays for your teammates.

In years past, most coaches and players regarded passing as the most important offensive fundamental. But basketball today is a high-scoring contest, and shooting dominates the game. So let's get going; we'll start with shooting.

## SHOOTING

The object of the game is to "put the ball through the hoop." Victory comes to the team which can score more often than its opponents; and scoring depends entirely upon shooting baskets. Passing, dribbling, cutting, and even the use of intricate scoring plays are valueless unless they result in putting the ball in the basket. A good shooting team has confidence. Marksmanship superiority will usually result in victory.

When a small boy attempts a shot, he gets as close to the basket as possible and then uses a lift motion in order to achieve the height necessary in getting the ball above the basket. This underhand method was first used for distance shooting. As guarding technique improved, the underhand shot developed into the "roll" or chest shot, which is popular in the South and West. Another type of shot which is gaining in usage and popularity dispenses with the roll and depends upon wrist- and knee-action for control and power.

It is probably true that all methods are equally correct and that the success of each depends upon the degree of concentration and practice. Persistent practice of any shooting method is certain to result in a degree of accuracy. Almost anyone can learn to shoot and, strange as it seems, people without normal vision oftentimes become expert marksmen. Shooting a basketball can be compared to firing a rifle; it is important to draw a bead on the target and then concentrate on that point before, during, and after the shot.

There are two basic types of shots, namely the "clean" shot and the "bank" shot. A clean shot means that the ball drops through the rim of the basket without striking the backboard. The player attempting the shot should concentrate only on the rim and try to drop the ball directly through the hoop. A backboard shot is, as the name implies, one which caroms off the backboard and into the basket. The player should aim at a certain spot on the backboard, depending upon his position on the floor. There are a great number of variations of the clean shot and the bank shot and they are discussed in this chapter. While a clean shot can be made from any point on the floor except directly under or behind the basket, this is not true of a bank shot. However, most players prefer the advantages which accompany the bank shot from certain spots.

## SHOOTING CHART

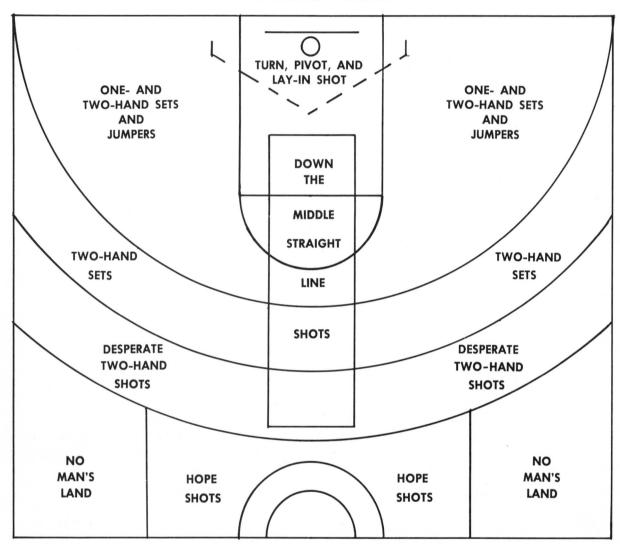

**LET'S NOT KID OURSELVES—THE BETTER SHOOTING TEAM WINS.** Good shooters know their areas and their shots. To be a great shooter requires hours of constant practice. A player can be helped by learning the shots and the areas in which they should be used, but if he does not pay the price — practice the right way and dedicate himself to daily practice—he will never be a great shot nor a great scorer. Start right and do it right!

# KNOW YOUR SPIN
*(English)*

In all shots spin plays an important part.
Today very few players throw a "dead" ball
(floater — little or no spin).

*Types of spin*
    REVERSE SPIN
    CARRY SPIN . . . . left and right
    LIFT SPIN . . . . left and right

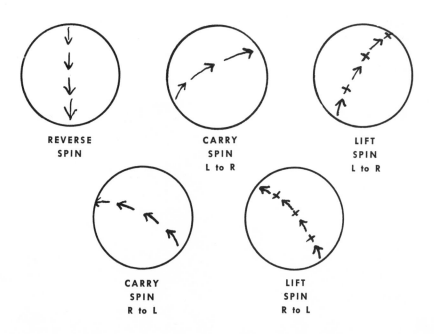

## Types of Spin

In all shots where use of the backboard is necessary, spin plays an important part. Spin may be "reverse," "carry," or "lift." Each of these three may be used when banking the ball at certain points on the board and all are influenced by the position of the player on the floor. Reverse spin is developed by releasing the ball from the tips of the fingers in such manner that it revolves toward the player. It requires considerable exaggeration. Carry spin is released with a turn of the hand designed to impart a spin from left to right or right to left. Lift spin is produced by an upward lift of the hand and fingers which develops a diagonal spin of the ball.

A great number of coaches eliminate spin altogether on close shots against the backboard. This permits a "softer" shot but requires direct angles for accuracy. The use of spin may permit a successful shot when a straight or direct angle is impossible.

In shooting, let's start with the *lay-up shot* — the one a fellow uses when he drives under or past the basket. If you are driving to the basket from a corner, lay the ball up against the backboard with an underhand sweep. Make a complete follow-through, carrying the ball as high up in the air as you can.

**UNDERHAND LAY-UP:** This was one of the original shots in basketball and is still used by many players when they have a clear path to the basket. The shooter carries the ball as high as possible before releasing it against the backboard. (Some players use this shot following a drive to the basket from the free-throw circle.)

**ONE-HAND OVERHAND LAY-UP:** The shooter takes off on a one-two slap of his feet on the floor and focuses his eyes on the spot on the backboard where he plans to bank the ball. On the right side of the basket, the "one" count is with the right foot and the "two" count is with the left foot, so that the shooter is releasing the ball from the hand opposite the foot last to hit the floor.

If you are driving across in front of the basket or toward the basket, use an overhand shot. No matter which side you are cutting past, you will want to shoot the ball with the hand which is away from the goal (and your opponent); thus, when shooting, you will take off on the foot opposite from your shooting hand. When shooting the lay-up with your right hand, take off on the left foot, and vice versa.

Go as high and as near to the basket as possible. When making a lay-up shot going under or close to the basket, pick a spot on the backboard and lay the ball gently on the spot. Don't use too much spin! Too much spin will carry the ball across the top of the basket and you'll miss an easy two-pointer.

**RUNNING ONE-HAND "DRAG" SHOT:** Note that the shooter is dragging the toe of his right shoe to slow down his progress and steady his body. (Please note the *concentration* of the boy's eyes on the target!) The ball is released with the arms and fingers fully extended and the right knee is usually brought up level with the belt.

Now, what about the *one-handers* from twenty-five and thirty or more feet from the goal? Well, maybe *you* can do it! But I don't believe the majority of fellows can shoot accurately with one hand from more than thirty feet from the basket. As a starter, let's just try some one-handers from the area of the free-throw circle. You come in fast and high and carry the ball up in front of the face or above the shoulder and release it from the finger tips. Then let's bend those same fingers out and down to get a good finish on the shot.

Oh, yes, you will take off from the floor on your opposite foot again and bring up the knee on the same side as the shooting hand as high as you can. If you will count "one — two" on the shot, your left foot will hit the floor on the "two" count and the right knee will come up just as you release the ball. It's a good shot, but be sure that your shoulders are square to the basket and that your eyes are focused on the front of the rim.

**ONE-HAND SET SHOT:** The youngster executing the true one-hand set in this illustration is giving a splendid demonstration of this valuable shot. He has advanced his right foot to meet the pass and almost as soon as the ball touches his hands, he has started to focus his eyes on the basket. Further, he has immediately turned the ball so that his shooting hand (the right) is on top and in back of the ball while his left hand holds it secure. Bringing his right foot back, he continues to concentrate on the target while he raises the ball to a position over his right shoulder. Here, his left hand pushes the ball back and drops away as the ball is raised slightly and released with a complete straight arm follow-through. The fingers maintain contact with the ball as long as possible before the wrist snap starts it on its way. Then, the fingers fall loosely down in a full-spread position.

Then there's a *one-hand set shot*. It is made just the same except that you are not in motion. Some players do raise the knee with the shot, and some take a step toward the basket as they release the ball. But it is not necessary to do more than stop, get your balance, aim the ball, and then release it with a good elbow, wrist, and finger follow-through. (The arm should be fully extended.) A snap of the knees helps.

## ONE-HAND SET SHOT

Tony Lavelli, Yale All-America star, 1949 and 1950, demonstrates in this continuous motion photo the correct form and technique used in the one-hand set shot. Tony was one of the greatest one-hand shooting artists in the history of the game, being equally adept in the use of the one-hand set, jumper and hook shots.

Note the use of the left hand in supporting and lifting the ball to a position over the right shoulder. As the right hand starts to move toward the basket, the left hand moves away in a free and relaxed motion. (Study the finish of the shot — right arm fully extended, fingers loose and apart following the "flip," the palm of the hand toward the basket accompanied by a snap of the knees and a slight leap from the floor.)

## One-Hand Jump Shot (Jumper)

The jump shot is the most popular shot in the game. Originally developed in the West, it gained popularity in the Middle West and in the East after Hank Luisetti (an All-America star with Stanford) made scoring history when his team played a number of games in the areas.

Every player uses the jump shot today and some players use it exclusively. It is a deadly scoring weapon within a reasonable distance from the basket, and, unless the opponent guarding the jump shooter is exceptionally tall, the shot is almost impossibe to stop.

The shot usually follows a dribble in which the player comes to a hard stop, brings his feet close together in a jumping position and then leaps straight up from the "stop" position. The leap gives maximum protection and is the chief

reason the shot is so hard to stop.

As the feet are brought together, the player should crouch to secure "explosive" power and, at the same time, quickly twist the ball so that his shooting hand is on top of the ball with the other hand acting as a support and guide. The ball should be quickly lifted to a position over the right shoulder and as high as the extended arm will permit. The left hand (right-handed shooter) should then force the ball back until the shooting hand is under the ball, with the palm facing directly upward. The elbow lifts the arm a little higher, and the wrist snaps the ball upward and forward as it is released with the fingertips.

The eyes should be concentrated on the center of the outside rim and kept focused there to insure a complete follow-through. This shot is the "must" in the shooting library of every player in the game.

## Two-Hand Set Shots

We got to it at last, didn't we? The *two-hand* set shot! It's a great shot. Fun, too. Like the fifty-yard pass in football.. It's much more accurate than the long one-handers and easily mastered. Now hold the ball just as you did when you made the chest pass, fingers spread wide and relaxed. (Never try to grip the ball.) In fact, the ball should be held so loosely that it would drop out of your hands if you moved your little fingers outward. That's it . . . *loose!*

We're ready to shoot, now. Lower the knees and let the ball drop down a couple of inches—with the wrists only, not with the arms! Then snap the knees back and spring from the floor, sending the ball with a natural spin toward the goal. The hands stay on the ball as long as possible and end up with palms toward the basket and close together. That's all there is to it. Two points.!

**TWO-HAND SET SHOT:** The player's eyes are watching the ball as it comes toward him and he has stepped forward with his left foot to "meet the pass." As soon as the ball is safely in his hands, he focuses his eyes on the target and raises the ball to a position just below eye level. While he concentrates on the target, he unlocks his wrists (dropping the ball slightly forward and downward). Now, he brings the ball up and coils his body for the power needed to carry the ball to the basket. Note that his feet have left the floor and that his hands have remained on the ball as long as possible. After the release of the ball, the hands remain close together with the fingers loosely spread in the position with which they grasped the ball before the shot. The shooter lands lightly on the balls of his feet, completing the smooth rhythm of the shot. (As in firing a rifle, the eyes remain focused "on target" *after* the bullet has sped on its way.)

**TWO-HAND OVERHEAD SET SHOT:** The overhead set shot is a favorite weapon of tall players. Here, the player is lifting the ball over his head as he focuses his eyes on the basket. At the same time, he has flexed his knees so that when he leaps he may have sufficient power to propel the ball the necessary distance. As he releases the ball, he takes a short step forward with his right foot and kicks his left foot back. The hands, held loosely together with the fingers spread, complete the follow-through. (Many big men dispense with the short step-skip and leap straight upward for this shot.)

**LEFT-HAND TURN SHOT:** Holding the ball at arm's length, the player pivots on his right foot. Continuing his turn, he releases the ball from his fully extended arm and hand and banks it into the basket.

**RIGHT-HAND HOOK SHOT:** The pivot player receives the ball, holds it at arm's length, focuses his eyes on the basket, and then takes his step and uses a full-arm hook shot to score.

**FAKE TURN INTO THE LANE AND RIGHT-HAND JUMP SHOT:** The pivot player is playing close to the area of the free-throw line. He fakes a right turn into the lane and then steps to his left and makes a one-hand jump shot. (Note the little hesitation while the player is in the air. This enables him to aim the ball accurately just before releasing it.)

**FAKE AND TURN INTO LANE FOR LEFT-HAND HOOK SHOT:** The pivot player is playing close to the area of the free-throw line. He fakes a right-hand shot, pivots quickly, drives into the lane, and hooks the ball with his left hand.

**INSIDE PIVOT AND DRIBBLE:** The pivot player is on the left side of the lane. He receives the ball, fakes a shot to raise his opponent's hands, swings the ball down to his left hip close to his stomach and pivots in toward his opponent. Then, transferring the ball to his right side, he dribbles with his right hand to the other side of the lane for the shot.

**UNDER AND AROUND WITH A VARIETY OF SHOTS:** The pivot player is on the right side of the lane. He pivots around, fakes a right-hand shot and then continues his dribble on under and around to the other side of the basket. Here, depending upon the situation, he may attempt a left-hand shot; a right-hand shot; a two-hand overhead; a right-hand turn; a left-hand turn, or a one-hand jump shot.

[ 63 ]

# FREE-THROW SHOTS

The free-throw is one of the game's most important shots. More games are probably won or lost on the free-throw line than in any other department of the game (this certainly applies to the close games).

The underhand shot is the most natural and the easiest. However, it is seldom used in a game, and a great many players prefer to use the shot they use in trying to score from the field — the one- or two-hand set and the "overhead" one- or two-hand set shot. However, I am sure you will use the shot in which you are most accurate, and if a change is to be made — leave it to your coach.

Players often get in the habit of bouncing the ball on the floor several times before they attempt a free-throw in order to relieve tension. This is fine, but the player should not make it a show-off stunt, *and* he should concentrate on the basket while bouncing the ball rather than look down in catching and flipping the ball.

This is the one shot which will improve with extensive practice no matter what method of shooting is used. Good free-shot shooters win the vital games — often in the last second of the game. Be a dead-eye from the free-throw line!

**TWO-HAND UNDERHAND FREE-THROW:** The player "on the line" is holding the ball just below the level of his eyes while he sights the target. Then, he lowers the ball at arm's length until it reaches the vicinity of his knees. As he lifts the ball, he unlocks his wrists to gain power. The shot is completed with the arms fully extended and his hands **make a complete follow-through with the palms facing the basket.** (Note that the shooter's back is held perfectly straight all through the shot.)

**ONE-HAND FREE-THROW:** The shooter holds the ball just below eye level and concentrates on the target. Dropping the ball slightly to loosen his wrists and secure leverage, he then lifts it with his left hand to a position over his right shoulder. Now, he presses the ball back with his left hand and then drops it away as he lifts the ball with his shooting hand (right). He propels the ball upward and forward and finishes with a wrist snap which flips the fingers through and after the ball which insures a full follow-through.

**TWO-HAND OVERHAND FREE-THROW:** The shooter is demonstrating with perfect form the two-hand overhand free-throw. He holds the ball just below the level of his eyes while he concentrates on the target. Note that the arms are held close to the body and when the wrists are unlocked, the ball drops slightly. Rising on his toes as he lifts the ball, he flips it smoothly toward the basket. The hands are close together with the palms facing the basket at the end of the shot.

**SHOW-OFF POSITION FOR FREE-THROW:** Some players stand to the extreme right or left of the free-throw line when attempting the penalty shot. There is no logic to this shot and the shooter would undoubtedly be just as accurate from a position directly in front of the basket. (And a lot less conspicuous.)

**TWO-HAND OVERHEAD FREE-THROW:** Tall players often prefer the two-hand overhead free-throw. The ball is held just below eye level while the shooter sights his target. Continuing his concentration on the target, the player lifts the ball (with two hands) up over his head. Some shooters unlock the wrists at this point by dropping the ball farther back. Others merely flip the ball forward from the overhead position. In either case, the finish is the same as in the two-hand overhand set-shot with the exception that the hands end up slightly higher. Note that the arms are close together and that the palms of the hands are facing the basket.

## Tip-Ins

The tip-ins are to basketball what the jab is to boxing — the soft-touch fancy tip maneuvering of a good player. Any team that possesses one or two "tip-in" artists can readily break the morale of its opponents.

The principal requisite of this type of shot is the desire to jump — and rejump. And with timing a player can be developed into a good tip-in artist. I have seen players only 5 feet 11 inches tall make tip-in shots against players who were 6 feet 6 inches; it's hard to believe, but it has been done.

One of the best exercises for developing into a tip-in artist is the Long Island University "wall drill tip-in drill" which was originated at the university with the aid of one of my players, Bob Smith. I took a ball and asked the player, to come into the hall. Giving the ball to Smith, I made him go through passing and tip-in maneuvers. Within a few minutes Smith was really tired.

In this exercise you must keep the ball moving up against the wall, never stopping, with the use of only your finger tips. Tap the ball against the wall and keep jumping. Should you tire, pause, and come to a stop; your jumping stops but you bring the ball down to shoulder-level and "beat" it against the wall — similar to a one-hand piano exercise. Again should you tire, switch hands in order to keep the ball moving. The ball must not stop or touch the floor. Boxing time is kept; three minutes of tip-in, one minute of rest. It's a tough test — but good players can do it.

## The Tip-In Shot

The tip-in shot is important to all players. Pivot men will have more opportunities for its use than other players, but all should try to master it. The shot may be made with both hands or with one. It is probably better to concentrate on two-hand practice at the beginning and then work on each hand. The ball should rest momentarily on the tips of the fingers to eliminate tapping or slapping and then is re-

leased by a slight snap of the wrists and fingers. The wall drill is excellent for teaching control. (The entire squad can work at one time.)

Earlier, you learned how to develop a "fingertip touch." Here it is put to use. The art of "tip-in" has lost some of its beauty in game play because boys have failed to pay the price in developing this important shot. It's an easy shot to make and an easy score results.

"Do you make this shot clean or use the board?" For the best result it is wise to use the board. A great deal depends upon the position of the player and the success of this shot depends upon the player's ability to control the ball at the height of his leap.

## BALL HANDLING

Teamwork depends almost entirely upon this vital part of basketball. It is much more important than any other phase of the game — even more important than banging away at the basket. Every coach tries to blend his players together so they can control the ball until a teammate can break free to a good shooting position or can be set up for a good, protected shot at the basket.

Big hands are an asset in handling the ball, but small hands are not a handicap. "Feel" and skill can be developed by practicing the various passes and learning how and when to use them. Accuracy and the elimination of waste motion in catching and passing the ball are the earmarks of a good passer. And, against good teams, fast passes are important in keeping the ball moving so that the opponents will not have time to move in a line between the ball and the basket.

Many players telegraph their passes by looking directly at their receivers. But the expert passer maintains a poker face, looking straight ahead and depending upon marginal or peripheral vision to locate the teammate who is in the best position to receive the pass. (You can develop this ability to see sideways while watching someone in front of you. Practice this off the court; look straight ahead and yet *see* on each side at the same time.) Mastery of the various passes will enable the passer to drive the ball to the open teammate at the right time and in the right position.

When passing aim the ball to your teammate between his belt and shoulders and, if the teammate is moving, he should be given a good lead. Good passers pass the ball at the right time to the right player in the right place. Tall players should rely upon the high passes— two-hand overhead, baseball, and the hook and "shot" passes. Shorter players will have more success with passes which are closer to the floor — the chest, one- and two-hand underhand, and the flip and bounce passes.

A mistake often made by the beginner is to place his palm on the ball. This is not good since the ball responds most effectively to finger-tip control. Developing this touch is important. In mastering the art of throwing (basketball, baseball, or football) a player *must* develop finger-tip touch.

A good player develops finger-tip touch by passing. This is the outcome of hard, long hours of practice.

The good athlete in most games usually possesses good hands and strong wrists. In basketball, the fingers and wrists dominate in controlling the ball. Almost any player can develop good hands, fingers, and wrists through special exercises. (Squeezing a handball time after time every day is an excellent method of developing strength, sensitiveness, and suppleness.)

### Catching the Ball

It doesn't seem possible that a fellow would have trouble catching a big round thing like a basketball. Yet, the amount of fumbling, lost motion, and loss of the ball in a single game because a player does not catch the ball is astonishing.

Now, when catching the ball, your first step is to move *toward* the ball. Be sure that the muscles of your arms, hands, and fingers are relaxed. Catch the ball with the hands in back of the ball and formed so that they make a soft pocket. Never let the ball hit the heels of your hands.

Watch the ball all the way into the pocket formed by the hands. Don't fight the ball and don't grab it! Just pick it out of the air with your finger tips, allowing your hands to give just enough to absorb the shock. "Keep your eye on the ball" is an axiom that is often heard in baseball, golf, football, tennis, handball, and in many other games. It is just as important in basketball. Since you can only do one thing at a time, the immediate and most important task is to *catch* the ball. If you can't catch the ball, you can't pass it!

Not all the fumbles are caused by failures to catch the ball. "Bad passes and fumbles go together!" But, from the point of view of the receiver, *concentration on catching the ball* will prevent many fumbles and/or loss of the ball even though the pass is bad. Be sure to watch out for spin on the ball. A spinning ball is hard to control as well as catch.

Make every effort to catch the ball with two hands. If it is necessary to go for the ball with one hand because of a bad pass, be sure to get the other hand on the ball as quickly as possible. And, familiarize yourself with the passes each of your teammates use. Some of your teammates may throw a hard, heavy ball, use excessive spin, or employ trick passes to such an extent that you, as well as the opponents, may be fooled.

## PASSING

Accurate passing comes through practice. Start with short, accurate passes. Then, speed them up. Here are a few don'ts: Don't hold the ball — keep it moving; don't try fancy passes; don't look one way and pass another; don't pass to a teammate's back; don't pass laterally across the court; don't telegraph your passes; don't "plug" a teammate (throw too hard); don't fool your teammate.

Before we discuss the most important passes, let's stress the importance of holding the ball so that only the pads of the fingers and the thumbs touch the ball. The ball should never touch the palms of the hands. Keep in mind that the ball is manipulated with the finger tips, wrists, forearms, and elbows in passing, shooting, and dribbling. Now, the passes.

## Two-Hand Chest Pass

The initial move is the same that is used in starting a dribble, a bounce pass, or a shot. The range of the pass is between ten and fifteen feet. Start the execution of the pass with the ball at the height of your chest. Then, the ball is permitted to drop just a trifle as you take a step forward and in the direction of the pass. The arms force the hands straight out as far as they will go and the snap of the elbows, accompanied by a flip of the wrists and fingers in which the thumbs turn under the ball, sends it spinning on its way. Some coaches require their players to start their set attack with two hands on the ball. This affords protection of the ball in a shot, dribble and, in the case of a pass, time to draw back the ball should the teammate for whom the pass was intended be covered by an opponent.

1. The two-hand chest pass is the most important pass in the game.
2. It is used more than any other pass in basketball.
3. This pass permits you to precede the actual pass with a fake.
4. It is a fast pass. You can catch the ball and pass with one motion.
5. It is the basic pass for all styles and systems of play.

**CHEST PASS:** Holding the ball chest-high with his fingers and thumbs spread, player 3 drops the ball slightly to unlock his wrists and then snaps the ball out in the same motion used in the two-hand set shot. The passer steps out with his left or right foot so that his body will be behind the pass. Observe that his arms have been snapped out straight and that his hands end up close together with the palms following the path of the ball.

**BASEBALL PASS:** "Lefty" 3 has carried the ball up to a position over his shoulder and is in the process of shifting his weight from the rear to the forward leg. His right hand is thrust forward to help maintain body balance. The throw resembles a catcher's throw to second base and the arm and hand snap out straight toward his teammate with the palm and the fingers of the throwing hand turning slightly toward the outside (left in this case) to eliminate excessive spin and the resulting curve.

## Baseball Pass

This is made just like a catcher's peg to second base. Bring the ball straight up and back to a position beside the ear. Don't wind up! From the position above the shoulder and beside the ear, the elbow is thrown straight out toward the objective and the forearm, hand, and fingers follow through as far as possible. The ball should be released as the weight shifts forward from the back leg and foot to the forward leg and foot. If necessary, turn the throwing hand to the outside at the end of the follow-through in order to eliminate the natural spin which will cause the ball to curve.

1. The baseball pass is the most important pass for distance.
2. It is most effective in starting the fast break.
3. It is an excellent pass with which to feed the pivot.
4. It is an excellent distance "lead" pass.
5. It is one of the fastest passes in the game.

## Two-Hand Overhead Pass

Hold the ball over the head with both hands and with the fingers well spread. It is important that the arms be kept straight so that you may gain as much height as possible. When ready to pass, take a short step forward and, at the same time, let the ball move an inch or two back by bending the wrists. Then, with a snap of the elbows, throw the wrists, hands and fingers through with the arms and hands extended toward the objective as far as possible. Throw the ball to your teammate on a high level; the receiver should catch it at arm's length above his head.

1. This pass makes a big man out of a little man!
2. It is difficult for the opponents to stop.
3. It is the best pass with which to feed the pivot.
4. It is an important give-and-go play pass.
5. It is a good fake to precede a dribble or a bounce pass.

**OVERHEAD PASS:** The passer has lifted the ball high over his head. Dropping the ball back to unlock his wrists, he snaps it forward while keeping his arms and hands close together during the follow-through. The ball may be passed on a direct line or plane or looped to clear the upraised hands of opponents.

## One- and Two-Hand Flip Passes

Make the underhand passes or "flips" with one or two hands. These passes may be forward, sideways, backward, or around the back. Release the ball with one or two hands almost as soon as it is received. Use your body to shield the ball no matter whether you use one or two hands or whether you pass the ball forward, laterally, backward or around the back.

1. One- and two-hand flip passes are extremely fast.
2. These passes are vital when a player is being pressed.
3. They blend in perfectly with the give-and-go offense.
4. Flip passes are a must when a team is "freezing" the ball.
5. These passes enable a team to keep the ball "hopping."

**BACK-FLIP PASSES:** This series show player 15 using one and two hands to flip the ball straight behind him to a teammate as well as flipping it over his shoulder. These passes are especially effective in "give-and-go" plays.

[ 77 ]

## The Bounce Pass

This can be thrown with one or two hands and in almost any direction. Snap or throw the ball with considerable force since contact with the floor eliminates some of its speed. Use this pass as a change-of-pace weapon and it should usually be preceded by some sort of a fake. Bounce passes can be used in almost any type of offense, but should be kept low. In terms of distance try to bounce the ball close to the receiver so he will catch it at a point no higher than the waist. Spin is not necessary for short passes, but on long bounce passes it will increase the speed of the ball.

1. The bounce pass is an effective weapon against zone defenses.
2. It is an excellent pass with which to feed the pivot player.
3. Back-bounce passes can be used in the give-and-go attack.
4. This pass is effectively used against the "press."
5. Following a fake, it is a good pass with which to feed cutters.

**BOUNCE PASS:** Player 23 is demonstrating but one of the bounce passes which are so effective in changing the plane of a team's passing pattern. Bounce passes may be made with one or two hands and thrown in practically any direction. Here, player 23 fakes to his left to bring his opponent's hands up. Then, the passer brings his left foot across for protection and bounces the ball to his teammate. Passer 23 is making the mistake of looking down instead of directly toward his teammate.

[ 78 ]

## Cross-Face and Cross-Body Passes

These are fast and vital to your game. These passes can be used efficiently while moving and are important because of that fact. Hold the ball loosely in your finger tips and throw it quickly. Some players become so proficient in the use of these passes that the ball barely comes to rest in their hands before it is again sent on its way. A full follow-through with the wrists, hands, and fingers is necessary, but the elbow action should be fast and short — almost like the action in the flip passes.

1. The cross-face and cross-body passes are extremely fast.
2. They are extremely deceptive when preceded by a fake.
3. Cross passes of all kinds are effective in the fast break.
4. These passes enable a cutter to rid of the ball quickly.
5. All types of cross passes blend in with the give-and-go offense.

**ONE-HAND CROSS-FACE PASS:** Player 15 is passing the ball to his left and over his left arm. This pass could be made high or low. It is often used deceptively by the feeder in a fast-break situation.

**ONE-HAND CROSS-BOUNCE PASS**: Here, the passer is using an underarm cross pass to bounce the ball to a teammate on his left. Like the preceding cross-face pass, it can be used effectively and deceptively by the feeder in a fast-break situation.

## The Hook Pass

This can be made from the floor or while in the air and is an excellent pass to use when your opponent is playing you close and you must pass the ball forward, sideways or back. Hold the ball in the chest-pass position at the start. Then, the body is turned slightly to the left or right and the ball is held with one hand from the fully extended arm. Throw the pass with a full-arm sweep and hooked behind the head, not over the head or in front of the face. This is a hard pass to master, but it is effective in almost any game or situation. The fingers

should not leave the ball until the throwing arm has been fully extended over the head. Then the wrist, hand, and fingers co-ordinate in a snap which imparts speed to the ball. Warning: The ball will dart toward the floor if too much finger snap is used.

1. It is an effective pass for the big man.
2. It is a good pass to use when you are closely guarded.
3. The fast break can be started frequently with this pass.
4. It can be used in the give-and-go offense.
5. It is a good pass with which to feed the pivot.

**HOOK PASS:** Player 23 is facing away from his receiver. He extends the ball to arm's length, protecting it with his left hand. He "hooks" the ball directly over his head with his fully extended right arm and follows through. This pass resembles a hook shot in technique and execution. The ball is usually thrown too hard and too much of a follow-through will direct it toward the floor. The ball may be thrown with one or two hands and with the feet on or off the floor.

5

4

3

1

2

The above list of passes are basic and are the most common types in use in all types or styles of basketball. Practically all these passes with the exception of the chest and the bounce passes may be made while the passer is in the air. In fact, it may be safely stated that every pass with the exception of the roll pass may be made while in the air.

There are a great many other passes which are variations of or have some relation to the basic passes and which are used by virtually every player at one time or another. A short review of these passes follows:

1. Tap Pass. This pass is made by quickly extending one or two hands and tapping the ball (while it is coming toward the receiver). Rebounders who are out of position often tap the ball to a teammate; give-and-go players often reach out and tap the ball back to the passer and then change direction and cut for the basket; and it is frequently used by a dribbler at the end of his dribble to enable him to cut away more rapidly from his opponent. It is probably safe to say that this pass should be used only by the experienced and more versatile player.

2. Fake-Shot Pass. In this pass, usually directed toward the pivot player or a teammate near the basket, the passer concentrates on the basket and apparently shoots for the goal. Actually, he loops the ball toward a teammate who is standing near or who is cutting to the basket. Since it is a slow pass, it should be used only when the basket area is clear and preferably after a good fake.

3. Roll Pass. This is an emergency pass only. Show-off players often use it to feed the pivot or to upset their opponent by rolling the ball between his legs. However, it is a slow, difficult pass to make safely and is hard to recover. You can probably do without this pass except when caught in an emergency.

4. The Lob Pass. Almost in the same category as the tap and roll passes is the lob pass. In the hands of an expert passer, the pass can be very effective. Usage by a beginner or average player in a dangerous situation may mean disaster. However, it is a fine pass to use when passing to a pivot man who is moving toward an open position near the basket or to a cutter who is driving toward an uncongested area. Use the lob pass cautiously because it lends itself to easy interception by the opponents.

## DRIBBLING

The dribble is important if used properly — which means it should be used as follows: to get out of trouble; to drive in for a basket; to bring the ball up-court when no quick-break situation is present; to advance the ball rapidly in the fast break when passing is impossible or dangerous; when no teammate is in position to receive the ball and the player with the ball needs time to set up a play; when meeting the pressing defense; and in freezing the ball.

Keep in mind that the ball can be passed from one position to another many times faster than a player can dribble the ball. So, make up your mind that *you are not* going to hamper your team's attack by "hogging" the ball through the selfish use of the dribble *when you can pass.*

*Dribbling takes practice!* A lot of it! Start the ball low and with a long bounce. Then, bend the body well forward and keep low. Let the tips of the wide-spread fingers of the dribbling hand, right or left, meet the ball on the up-bounce with a slight give of the hand. Almost instantly, the fingers should push or press the ball back toward the floor. Try it slowly, standing still, and you will soon get the hang of it.

The ball is controlled by the fingers, which should be held slightly stiff with the wrist and arm fully relaxed. After you have learned to control the ball standing still, start to walk slowly forward, backward, to the right and to the left, keeping your head up and your eyes focused straight ahead. At the same time, practice your split vision — try to see everything ahead and to each side of you without turning the head.

You are now ready to start more rapid movement and you should crouch over and use a lower bounce which means more control. Dribbling around a chair or on the porch where the quarters are cramped is excellent for developing control of the ball. Sitting on a chair and dribbling the ball around it by using both hands is still another way to improve your dribbling control.

It is important that you learn to use your body to protect the ball and you can do this only if you learn to dribble with the left as well as the right hand. (If you can't dribble — your opponent will rush you every time you get the ball.)

Dribbling is undoubtedly next to shooting and passing in importance to the basketball player. The good dribbler can dribble at full speed; change direction; use the change of pace, the protection dribble, the hesitation, the crossover (both in forward and rear position), the double-time (going down and meeting the ball just as it leaves the floor); use either hand equally well, behind the back and through the legs; and accompany all this with feints and fakes of the head, shoulders, eyes and feet.

As in every other skill in basketball, you must put in hours of practice. Again — it's "pay the price." No player ever became outstanding without practice. Bob Cousy of the Boston Celtics practiced these skills day after day, over and over, thousands of times, year around. How about you?

**GOOD DRIBBLING FORM:** Player 23 is controlling the ball with his fingers fully spread and is keeping the ball low (high bounces are easily intercepted). Note that his head is up and his eyes are focused straight ahead so that he may take advantage of any situation which may develop. He is however, dribbling the ball a little too far away from his body. Note the finger-tip control, the low bounce, the leg protection, the lifted head and the extended left hand for balance and protection.

**GOOD CONTROL AND FORM:** The player can retreat, pivot around to protect the ball, or advance quickly.

**ONE-HAND CONTROL:** This is a fine drill to control the ball with one hand. Note that the player in this series of pictures carries his left hand behind him, scoops the ball up with his right hand, and begins his dribble. This drill should always be performed at full speed.

### DRIBBLE AND TWO-HAND UNDERHAND SHOT:

The dribbler in this series is advancing rapidly toward the basket, keeping the ball low, controlling it with his finger tips, has his head up and his eyes focused ahead. At the conclusion of his dribble, he gathers the ball in and attempts a two-hand driving underhand lay-up shot.

**BASELINE DRIVE:** In this illustration, the corner man receives the ball, fakes to pass or dribble to the outside, and then dribbles along the baseline with his left hand. If his path to the basket is blocked, he will stop and go up for a one-hand jump shot as shown.

**MOVING AND SET SCREENS:** In this series, offensive players in black, 12 and 15, combine in demonstrating three of the most important screening moves in basketball. In the first illustration, player 15 is executing an "inside" screen (moving between his teammate 12 and his defensive opponent in white, also 12). Defensive player 23 is moving with his offensive opponent (15) and is keeping between him and the basket.

In the second illustration, offensive player 15 has moved behind his teammate's guard (white 12) in his execution of an outside screen.

In the third illustration, offensive player 15 has established a set screen behind his teammate's opponent (12). Player 15 must not move his feet, arms, or body or obstruct the movement of the defensive player (12) and must establish his set screen at least three feet from that player.

# CUTTING AND SCREENING

The player who *"moves"* is an important asset to any type of offense. Players who do something "without" the ball are invaluable but, strange as it seems, are few and far between. Most players want the ball so they can dribble, shoot, or drive for the basket. So they stand around and wait or call for the ball and contribute nothing to their team's offense and, in fact, become an obstruction on the court.

If you really want to be a good basketball player, school yourself to do something *without the ball.* Get into the team "circulation" and cut or screen so your teammates may get help from your moves. However, you must learn that there is more to cutting than running in a straight line at full speed. You must learn change of pace (moving slowly and then putting on a burst of speed or vice versa), change of direction, and sudden starts, stops and pivots.

The cutter must keep in mind that it is not always possible for a teammate to pass the ball to him when he cuts. Here is where timing comes in (the ability to move when a teammate is in a position to pass the ball).

Screening is important to the offense of every team. The player who knows how to screen for a teammate is invaluable. It is your responsibility to learn the various kinds of screens — inside, outside, and back (set and moving). Work at it! It's fun to execute a screen so efficiently that a teammate can get a good shot away or break free for an easy score. And you'll get a big kick out of his slap on the back and grin of thanks.

## SCREENS

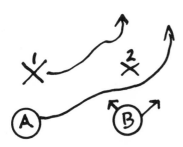

**INSIDE SCREEN.** Player A cuts between his teammate (B) and his teammate's opponent. Teammate B may cut to the right or to the left, using A's move as a screen.

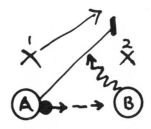

**SET OUTSIDE SCREEN.** Player A passes the ball to teammate B and moves to a position behind defensive player X2. Here, A sets a screen in a position so he may face the basket. Teammate B dribbles in for a shot.

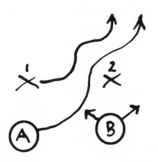

**OUTSIDE SCREEN.** Player A cuts as before but changes direction at the last moment and moves behind teammate B's opponent.

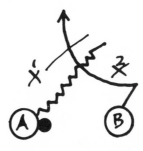

**DRIBBLE SCREEN.** Player A dribbles the ball to an outside set screen position behind teammate B's opponent (X2). Facing the basket, he will pass the ball to B if he breaks free.

# RATING CHART
## OFFENSE

POINT RATING: Superior—10  Excellent—9  Good—8  Fair—7  Poor—6  Weak—5

| ACTIVITY | WEEK | 1 | 2 | 3 | 4 | 5 | 6 | 7 | 8 |
|---|---|---|---|---|---|---|---|---|---|
| ABILITIES, GENERAL | | | | | | | | | |
| Condition | | | | | | | | | |
| Co-ordination | | | | | | | | | |
| Drive | | | | | | | | | |
| Jumping | | | | | | | | | |
| Reflexes | | | | | | | | | |
| Speed | | | | | | | | | |
| GAME SKILLS | | | | | | | | | |
| Body Balance | | | | | | | | | |
| Ball-Handling | | | | | | | | | |
| Catching Ball | | | | | | | | | |
| Faking | | | | | | | | | |
| FOOTWORK | | | | | | | | | |
| Starts | | | | | | | | | |
| Stops | | | | | | | | | |
| Feinting | | | | | | | | | |
| Pivots | | | | | | | | | |
| CUTTING | | | | | | | | | |
| Timing | | | | | | | | | |
| Change of Pace | | | | | | | | | |
| Change of Direction | | | | | | | | | |
| Circulation | | | | | | | | | |
| PASSING (one and two hand) | | | | | | | | | |
| Chest Pass (two hands) | | | | | | | | | |
| Baseball Pass | | | | | | | | | |
| Hook Pass | | | | | | | | | |
| Cross Face and Body | | | | | | | | | |
| Bounce Pass | | | | | | | | | |
| Overhead Pass | | | | | | | | | |
| Two-Hand Overhead | | | | | | | | | |
| Flip Passes | | | | | | | | | |
| Underhand Passes | | | | | | | | | |
| Outlet Pass | | | | | | | | | |
| Deception | | | | | | | | | |

(Continued)

| ACTIVITY | WEEK | 1 | 2 | 3 | 4 | 5 | 6 | 7 | 8 |
|---|---|---|---|---|---|---|---|---|---|
| DRIBBLING | | ...... | ...... | ...... | ...... | ...... | ...... | ...... | ...... |
| Speed | | ...... | ...... | ...... | ...... | ...... | ...... | ...... | ...... |
| Protection | | ...... | ...... | ...... | ...... | ...... | ...... | ...... | ...... |
| Ambidexterity | | ...... | ...... | ...... | ...... | ...... | ...... | ...... | ...... |
| Change of Direction | | ...... | ...... | ...... | ...... | ...... | ...... | ...... | ...... |
| Change of Pace | | ...... | ...... | ...... | ...... | ...... | ...... | ...... | ...... |
| REBOUNDING | | ...... | ...... | ...... | ...... | ...... | ...... | ...... | ...... |
| SCREENING | | ...... | ...... | ...... | ...... | ...... | ...... | ...... | ...... |
| Inside Screen | | ...... | ...... | ...... | ...... | ...... | ...... | ...... | ...... |
| Outside Screen | | ...... | ...... | ...... | ...... | ...... | ...... | ...... | ...... |
| Set Screen | | ...... | ...... | ...... | ...... | ...... | ...... | ...... | ...... |
| Dribble Screen | | ...... | ...... | ...... | ...... | ...... | ...... | ...... | ...... |
| SHOOTING | | ...... | ...... | ...... | ...... | ...... | ...... | ...... | ...... |
| One-Hand Shots | | ...... | ...... | ...... | ...... | ...... | ...... | ...... | ...... |
| Set | | ...... | ...... | ...... | ...... | ...... | ...... | ...... | ...... |
| Running | | ...... | ...... | ...... | ...... | ...... | ...... | ...... | ...... |
| Jumper | | ...... | ...... | ...... | ...... | ...... | ...... | ...... | ...... |
| Two-Hand Shots | | ...... | ...... | ...... | ...... | ...... | ...... | ...... | ...... |
| Straight Set | | ...... | ...... | ...... | ...... | ...... | ...... | ...... | ...... |
| Overhead | | ...... | ...... | ...... | ...... | ...... | ...... | ...... | ...... |
| Lay-Up | | ...... | ...... | ...... | ...... | ...... | ...... | ...... | ...... |
| Lay-Up Shots | | ...... | ...... | ...... | ...... | ...... | ...... | ...... | ...... |
| Bank | | ...... | ...... | ...... | ...... | ...... | ...... | ...... | ...... |
| Post Shot | | ...... | ...... | ...... | ...... | ...... | ...... | ...... | ...... |
| Pivot Shots | | ...... | ...... | ...... | ...... | ...... | ...... | ...... | ...... |
| Left Hand Shooting | | ...... | ...... | ...... | ...... | ...... | ...... | ...... | ...... |

CHIEF OFFENSIVE WEAKNESSES

# CHAPTER V

# DEFENSE FUNDAMENTALS

Now let's talk a little about defense. Playing on the offense may be more fun, but without defense there is no game. Defense can be fun, too, if you are a real competitor. Think of it as an individual battle you can wage with your opponent in trying to keep him from scoring. It is obvious that your opponent can run forward faster than you can run backward. Naturally, you will be closer to your opponent's basket when you are on the defense, but the attacking player has most of the other advantages in the race to get to the goal.

When on the defense, you must keep your weight back and balanced so that you can move quickly in any direction. When your opponent is quite a distance from the basket, you should play him "loose." As soon as he gets the ball you should "tighten up," but not so close to him that he can drive around you. When he gets close to the basket, you must play him tight. But don't foul him.

When your opponent has the ball a little distance from the basket and he is facing the goal, beware of his feints and attempts to get you off balance. You can best guard against this by keeping your eyes on him at all times. A great many coaches tell their players to watch their opponents' hips or belt buckles. Others prefer that a defensive player concentrate on the opponent's eyes and wait for him to make the first move. Some coaches tell their players to watch their opponents' knees. But *all* are agreed on one point — never turn your head! That doesn't mean that you can't watch the ball and the maneuvers of the other players. You can do that without turning your head through the use of peripheral vision.

But this peripheral, marginal, or side vision is valueless unless you can handle your feet. That's where rope jumping, heavy-bag punching, shadow boxing, and so on comes in. Keep your feet comfortably apart, one forward and one back in a boxer's stance, with the knees flexed and with the weight on the balls of the feet. Now, here's a big *secret!* Keep your weight *back* toward the goal behind so you can move quickly backward. Want to try something? All right, shift your weight to the right. Now, try to go to your left. You can't do it, can you? Not until you shift your weight to the left. Mean anything to you? Sure it does. It means that when you keep your weight back, you are prepared to move instantly toward the point you are guarding — the goal.

Now, you're ready to do a good job of guarding — ready to move with your opponent in any direction. If he goes to his left, you'll move to your right, using a boxer's glide with the right foot moving first to the right, followed by the left foot. Then the right foot will move to the right again followed by the left foot. Try not to cross the left foot over or across in front of the right. In fact, a good guard seldom, if ever, crosses his feet while on the defense near the basket.

Oh, yes, the arms. Keep your arms up and

your hands moving. One arm and hand is toward the opponent and the other is to the side. Move them, too. That distracts your opponent.

Yes, there's a lot more to individual defense. There's knowledge of the different methods of guarding the shooter, the cutter, and the dribbler as well as the man out of bounds. Stand sideways when you guard the out-of-bounds opponent so you can watch him as well as the court; guarding an opponent on the pivot and playing between him and the ball, shifting from side to side with the movement of the ball and playing in front of him in some instances is a skill the little fellow must master as well as the taller boy. Going front, sliding, and switching are other important man-to-man defensive skills you *must know* how to execute swiftly and surely.

## In-Line Principle

The basic principle of the man-to-man defense is for each player to stay between his opponent and the basket. This is known as the in-line principle and is used by all coaches employing the man-to-man defense. There are times, however, when variations of the in-line principle may be used. These will be explained in the chapter devoted to Team Defenses.

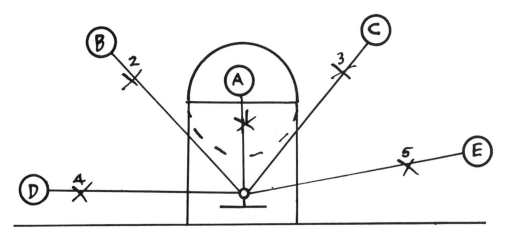

**IN-LINE PRINCIPLE.** Defensive players, X1, X2, X3, X4, and X5 are playing between their opponents, offensive players A, B, C, D and E, in a straight line between them and the basket they are defending.

## Front, Slide, Switch

In the man-to-man defense, the coach usually matches his best defensive players against his opponents' best offensive players. Thus, the coach sometimes matches speed against speed, and height against height. Yet, no matter how well the coach matches his defensive players against the opponents, there comes a time in every game when the opponents will use screens (set and moving) or the high or low post as mediums of freeing teammates from their guards. In such cases, defensive players find it impossible to stick with their assigned opponents. The front — slide — switch is then used to meet these offensive measures.

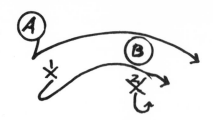

**FRONT.** Defensive player X1 is sticking with his opponent (A) by going in front of opponent B.

**SLIDE.** Defensive player X1 finds it impossible to go "front" to keep up with his opponent (A), so he "slides" between opponent B and his teammate X2 and manages to stick with him.

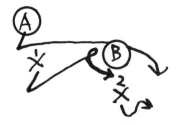

**SWITCH.** Defensive player X1 tries to stick with his opponent (A), but is caught by opponent B's screen. Defensive player X2 sees that his teammate X1 is screened away from A and calls "Switch!" Defensive players X1 and X2 now "trade" opponents (temporarily).

## Defensive Roll

When a defensive player is trapped by an offensive screen (set or moving) or by a post block, one of his teammates usually "switches" to cover the freed opponent. In this case, the trapped defensive player may find it neccessary to use the defensive roll in order to help out with the defense and particularly to cover the opponent of the teammate who has switched.

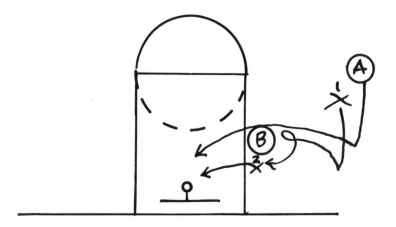

**DEFENSIVE ROLL.** Offensive player A has cut to the left, changed direction and cut across in front of the offensive pivot player (B). Defensive player X1 is forced into the set screen established by opponent B. Defensive player X2 sees that his teammate (X1) is trapped and calls "Switch!" He then switches to cover opponent A. Defensive player X1 immediately uses the "defensive roll" to cover opponent B.

## Boxing-Out

Lazy defensive players often forget to "box-out" their opponents, with the result that the other team frequently capitalizes on the grievous mistake and scores an easy basket. In the man-to-man defense, it is the responsibility of each defensive player to see that his particular offensive opponent (or a free opponent) does not have a free path to follow a shot and "double-up" the rebound for a two pointer.

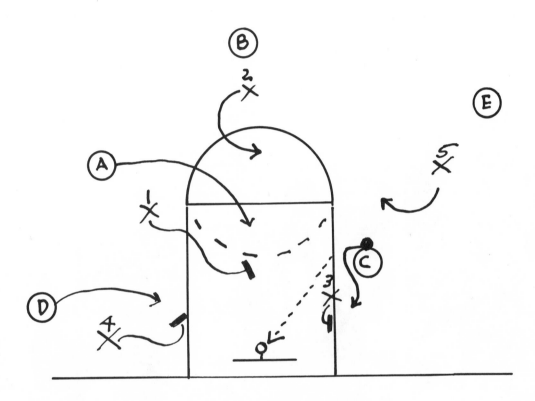

**BOXING-OUT.** Here, offensive player C takes a shot. Offensive teammates A and D (along with the shooter C), attempt to "follow-in" for a "tip-in" opportunity or to get the ball back for another shot. However, defensive players X1, X4, and X3, have used "boxing-out" techniques (moving between their respective opponents and the basket) to keep them from the ball. Note that defensive players X2 and X5 have retreated toward the basket a short distance for possible "deep" rebounds but they are not taking their eyes off of their respective opponents (B and E).

**DEFENSIVE REBOUNDING:** When rebounding, stand squarely facing the basket. Your feet should be placed in a fairly wide stance with the weight on the balls of the feet. Spread your fiingers, bring your elbows up and extend them out to your sides as far as possible. Take up as much room as you can and then leap up and slightly forward (as the ball starts down) to the height which represents your greatest leap. Good timing here is vital. Try to catch the ball so that one hand is next to the backboard and the other is in the rear of the ball away from the basket. This will prevent an opponent from knocking the ball out of your hands from the rear. (Your hand will be between your opponent's hand and the ball.) If you can't jump — you can't get rebounds. And — if you can't get rebounds — you'll probably sit on the bench!

# RATING CHART
## DEFENSE

| ACTIVITY | WEEK | 1 | 2 | 3 | 4 | 5 | 6 | 7 | 8 |
|---|---|---|---|---|---|---|---|---|---|
| BODY BALANCE — STANCE | | ...... | ...... | ...... | ...... | ...... | ...... | ...... | ...... |
| BLOCKING-OUT | | ...... | ...... | ...... | ...... | ...... | ...... | ...... | ...... |
| FOOTWORK | | ...... | ...... | ...... | ...... | ...... | ...... | ...... | ...... |
| GUARDING OPPONENT (General) | | | | | | | | | |
| Guarding Passer | | ...... | ...... | ...... | ...... | ...... | ...... | ...... | ...... |
| Guarding Cutter | | ...... | ...... | ...... | ...... | ...... | ...... | ...... | ...... |
| Guarding Dribbler | | ...... | ...... | ...... | ...... | ...... | ...... | ...... | ...... |
| Guarding Scorer | | ...... | ...... | ...... | ...... | ...... | ...... | ...... | ...... |
| Guarding Out-of-Bounds Player | | ...... | ...... | ...... | ...... | ...... | ...... | ...... | ...... |
| Guarding the Big Man | | ...... | ...... | ...... | ...... | ...... | ...... | ...... | ...... |
| REBOUNDING | | ...... | ...... | ...... | ...... | ...... | ...... | ...... | ...... |
| DEFENSIVE TALKING | | ...... | ...... | ...... | ...... | ...... | ...... | ...... | ...... |
| USE OF HANDS | | ...... | ...... | ...... | ...... | ...... | ...... | ...... | ...... |
| OVERSHIFTING | | ...... | ...... | ...... | ...... | ...... | ...... | ...... | ...... |
| FRONT-SLIDE-SWITCH | | ...... | ...... | ...... | ...... | ...... | ...... | ...... | ...... |
| BAD HABITS | | ...... | ...... | ...... | ...... | ...... | ...... | ...... | ...... |
| Crossing Feet | | ...... | ...... | ...... | ...... | ...... | ...... | ...... | ...... |
| Turning Head | | ...... | ...... | ...... | ...... | ...... | ...... | ...... | ...... |
| Lowering of Arms | | ...... | ...... | ...... | ...... | ...... | ...... | ...... | ...... |
| Lateral Movement | | ...... | ...... | ...... | ...... | ...... | ...... | ...... | ...... |
| Moving Backward | | ...... | ...... | ...... | ...... | ...... | ...... | ...... | ...... |
| Shifting Weight | | ...... | ...... | ...... | ...... | ...... | ...... | ...... | ...... |
| Defensive Roll | | ...... | ...... | ...... | ...... | ...... | ...... | ...... | ...... |

CHIEF DEFENSIVE WEAKNESSES

## CHAPTER VI

# TEAM OFFENSES

Ninety per cent of all teams use the fast break as a part of their offensive system. Because of this fact, most coaches will try to coordinate the fast break with one or more set offenses. Since you are using this book to get ready to "make the team" it is neccessary only to give you a brief introduction to the various types of offenses, since the choice of an offense rests solely with the coach.

### THE FAST BREAK

The first objective of the fast break is, naturally, to advance the ball into scoring territory as quickly as possible. The second objective is to secure a two-on-one, three-on-two, or a four-on-three advantage against the opponents. There are a number of advantages in the use of the fast break but the chief one is to secure a quick score through outnumbering. A second major advantage lies in the fact that a team which is efficient in the use of the fast break will force the opponents to curtail their offense since it will be necessary for them to keep one or more players back to stop the "break."

It is important that the ball be placed in play as soon as it is obtained through a rebound, interception, blocked shot, or fumble. Then, through passing the ball forward and filling three imaginary lanes of the court (middle, left side and right side), the ball should be advanced with great speed by means of fast passes from one player to another. In some cases it may be necessary for the "middle" player to dribble the ball as he and his two "wing" teammates advance deep into scoring territory.

In most uses of the fast break, the middle man stops at the free-throw line unless there is a clear path to the basket. The left and right side "wing" players scoot down the sidelines and then converge on the basket. The player who is unguarded (three-on-two situation) will receive the ball for the shot.

The middle man often ends up with the ball on the free-throw line unguarded. In this case, he should attempt the shot. And, should the defensive players stop the "break" by good defensive work, it is often possible to pass the ball to a fourth teammate (trailer) who follows the first wave and then breaks late into scoring territory. The rebounder usually follows up-court more slowly to take care of his team's defense should the ball be fumbled or intercepted.

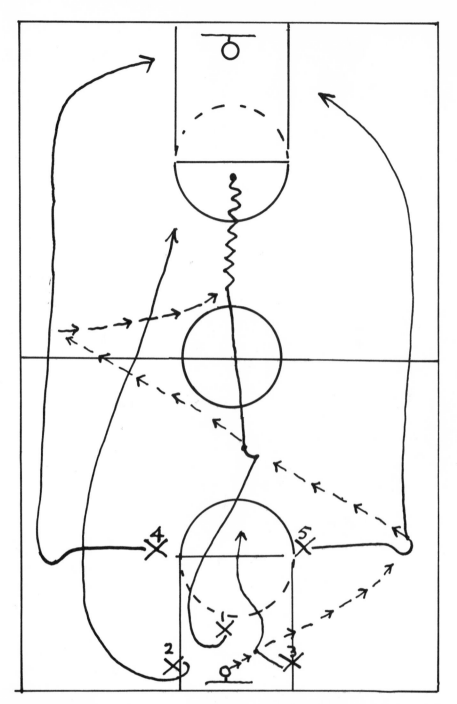

**FAST BREAK TECHNIQUE.** Defensive players X1, X2, and X3 form the rebound triangle and X3 makes the rebound. He immediately passes the ball (outlet pass) to teammate X5 on the right sideline. Player X1 turns and sees that teammate X4 (left-wing man) has taken the left sideline lane, so he cuts up the center of the court to take the middle man position. Player X5 passes the ball to X1, who passes in turn to X4, the left-wing man. X4 passes the ball back to the middle man (X1), who now dribbles at full speed to the free-throw line where he stops. The wing men now converge on the basket and X1 will pass to the open player, shoot, or turn and pass to the trailer (teammate X2) who has followed in the second wave of the "break." The rebounder, X3, has followed slowly up court to become the "safety" man.

[ 99 ]

## THE FAST BREAK

The climax of the fast break is shown on the blackboard. The "middle" man (1) has dribbled to the free-throw line and stopped. If unguarded, he will shoot. If challenged by an opponent, he will pass to the teammate who is free. Here, he passes to teammate 3 on the right. Player 3 has passed the ball back to the trailer (4) who is breaking into the lane. The rebounder (5) is advancing slowly to take care of the back court defense.

Here, we have a fast break "three-on-two" situation. The middle man (25) is dribbling hard up the center of the court. The trailer is behind the right wing player (23) and the rebounder (24) is advancing slowly to take care of the defense.

The dribbler (25) has stopped on the free-throw line and is faking a shot to draw out one of the defensive players (15). Note that the defensive teammate (12) is dropping back under the basket.

Defensive player 15 challenges the middle man (25) and the ball is passed to the right wing teammate (23) who is cut-

Right wing fast break player 23 throws a hard stop, gets his balance, and prepares to shoot. Defensive player 12 now starts out to stop the shot. The right-wing player is preparing to shoot but he notes that his left-wing teammate (12 — white jersey) is still coming (extreme right).

Defensive player 12 has moved out to guard the right-wing offensive player 23. The middle man holds his position on the free-throw line. (Note the left-wing fast-break player on the extreme right side of the court).

Defensive player 12 has moved close to fast-break player 23 (with the ball). Now the left wing fast-break teammate (12 — white jersey) cuts behind defensive players 12 and 15 and is free under the basket. Player 23 uses the bounce pass to get the ball to teammate 12 for the easy under-the-basket shot.

ing along the right sideline and toward
he basket.

## CIRCULATION

The "deep figure 8" is the basis of most attacks, and the "five-man give-and-go" circulation which is diagrammed and explained in this chapter often serves as an offense in itself. Usually, however, it is used as the basis of setting up plays built around the use of a post (a player stationed in the outer half of the free-throw circle), or a pivot (a player stationed close to the basket). Other circulations follow certain patterns which are designed to set up plays and provide defensive balance (players in the back court to quickly oppose opponents should they secure the ball).

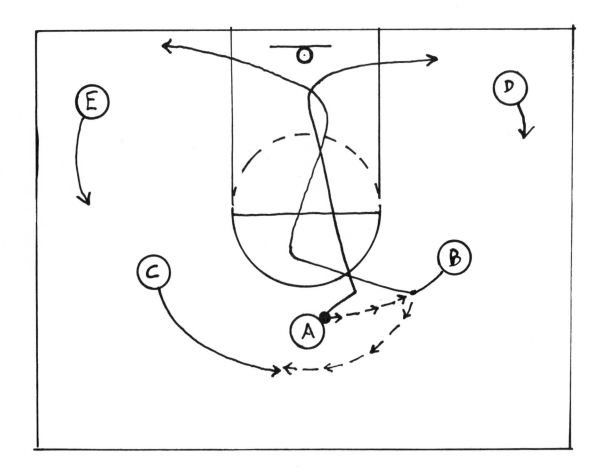

**FIVE MAN GIVE-AND-GO CIRCULATION.** Player A passes the ball to teammate B and cuts toward the basket. Correct procedure would require him to extend his left hand above his head for a target should B give him a return (give-and-go) pass. Player B now passes the ball to C and also cuts toward the basket. Note that player A cuts to the right corner (because he passed the ball to his right) and player B cuts to the left corner (because he passed the ball to his left). Player C will pass to teammate D, and D will pass to E, and the pass and cut (give-and-go) will continue.

**GIVE-AND-GO WEAVE IN ACTION**

## POST ATTACKS

The use of a strong, tall player with good feeding and scoring ability is the basis of this attack. The big man is stationed in the outer half of the free-throw circle and his teammates use him as a set screen or "post" around which they can cut in order to get away from their opponents. Most post attacks today use a "moving" or shifting post player so he may have less difficulty in breaking away from his opponent. The post player often breaks out from deep territory to the ball to set up plays for teammates or to attempt a personal drive to the basket for a shot.

## PIVOT ATTACKS

The pivot attack is used much in the same way as the post attack except that the big man operates close to the basket and on the sides of the free-throw lane. It is assumed that the pivot player will be a scorer who can use a variety of turn, pivot, hook, and jump shots with which to score. In addition, he becomes a feeder when he cannot shoot or when his teammates set up a play and break free and toward the basket. As in the use of the post player, most coaches expect the pivot player to keep moving from one side of the free-throw lane to the other or to break out to the ball.

[ 103 ]

## HELD BALL SITUATIONS

Held ball situations will occur between ten and twenty times a game, and it is important to a team's success that the ball be obtained. Here, good leaping ability on the part of all members of the team pays off. Plays are possible from held-ball situations, but most coaches today are content to secure possession of the ball.

**HELD-BALL FORMATION:** The ball is being tossed up by the official in the white team's front-court circle following a held-ball situation in the front court. Note the leaping positions of the jumpers. They will leap up and then turn in toward the ball and try to tap it after it reaches its highest point. The defensive players under the basket are playing behind their respective opponents. Keep in mind that only the jumping players are permitted inside the circle. The other players must remain outside the circle until the ball is tapped.

## OUT-OF-BOUNDS SITUATIONS

Scoring plays develop frequently from the out-of-bounds situations, but better results by far are obtained when the ball is out of bounds under a team's basket than when it is out of bounds on the side of the court. To be successful, out-of-bounds formations should be set up quickly and run off without hesitation.

In all such plays, however, it is wise to have certain players designated as safety receivers to insure protection for the ball should a play not be successful. The player who takes the ball out-of-bounds is the key to the success of the play and should be the best ball-handler on the team.

**OUT-OF-BOUNDS PLAYS:** The plays diagrammed here on the blackboards are popular and effective. In the first diagram, the player with the ball out of bounds must put the ball into play within five seconds. This means that the players must know their assigned positions and get to them quickly. Player 1 has the ball out of bounds near the free-throw lane and the play starts when he gives a signal such as slapping the ball or raising it over his head. Player 2 moves backward as shown. Player 4, farthest from the ball, holds his position until teammate 3 cuts around in back of player 5. Then player 4 fakes left, cuts into the lane, changes direction as shown, and cuts toward the ball. Player 5 moves straight back after the cutters have cut by him for a safety pass.

The second diagram shows a popular formation in which four men line up side by side across the lane. On a signal by the player out of bounds with the ball (1), they cut as shown.

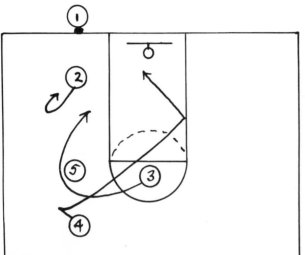 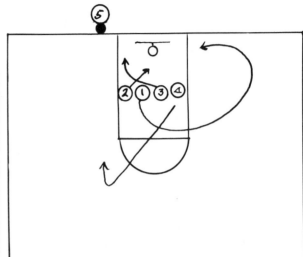

**OUT-OF-BOUNDS PLAY.** Player 1 has the ball out-of-bounds. He gives a signal by slapping the ball or raising it above his head and his teammates cut as follows: Players 2 and 3 start simultaneously as shown. Player 4 starts slowly left behind the screen by teammate 3, changes direction, cuts hard toward the right side of the basket, changes direction again near the right free-throw lane line and drives hard toward the basket. Player 3 continues on around 5 as shown. Player 5 waits until teammates 3 and 4 have cleared behind him and then drops straight back for a safety pass.

**OUT-OF-BOUNDS PLAY.** Player 5 has the ball out of bounds and gives a signal to start the play. Player 1 circles out of the lane and to the right as shown. As soon as he has left, teammate 2 cuts through the hole and toward the basket and is immediately followed by teammate 3 who cuts toward the ball. Player 4 waits until all teammates have cleared and then cuts toward the back court for the safety pass.

# CHAPTER VII

# TEAM DEFENSES

## MAN-TO-MAN DEFENSE

The man-to-man defense was the original defense envisioned by Dr. James A. Naismith, the inventor of the game. Dr. Naismith said in one of his original thirteen rules of basketball: "Stick to your man like glue. Play him so closely that he will not be able to receive or pass the ball." This rule just about defines the man-to-man defense. Coaches match players, and every effort is made to stick with the assigned opponent on a man-to-man basis. If a screen or block of some kind prevents the assigned player from sticking with his opponent, then his teammates help him by switching.

The use of over-shifting, sagging, floating, and the front — slide — switch technique are important "team" measures which must be employed in order to have a good man-to-man team defense. Although it is good defensive play to try to watch the ball as well as the assigned opponent, the player is the chief target.

Front — slide — switch has been explained under Defense Fundamentals. A brief description of overshifting, sagging, floating, and the development of the rebound triangle will be presented in this chapter.

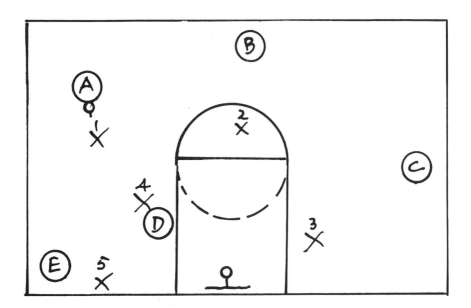

**OVERSHIFTING, SAGGING, FLOATING.** Here we find player X1, guarding the opponent with the ball (A), overshifting to his left (offensive player A evidently cannot go or dribble to his left). Defensive player X2 is sagging back from his opponent (B), while defensive teammate X3 is floating away from his opponent (C).

These moves — overshifting, sagging and floating — are "team" maneuvers to help with team defense. Note that defensive player X4 is playing "in front" of the pivot opponent (D). Defensive player X5 is overshifting toward the baseline, since it is a cardinal rule never to give the opponent room to cut along the baseline.

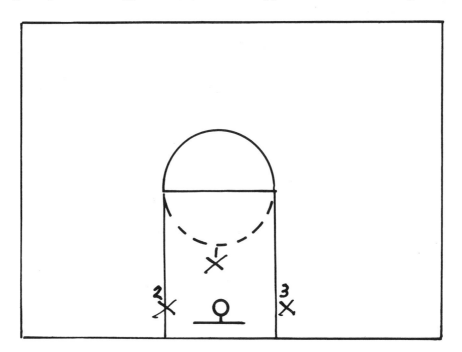

**REBOUND TRIANGLE.** Defensive players have formed the rebound triangle in front of their defensive basket. This principle is nearly always used in zone defenses, and most coaches like to develop this when using man-to-man defense. As can be seen, the dangerous points through which the offensive opponents may drive are blocked. The defensive players can shift right or left to keep opponents from breaking through. Following a shot, the players closest to the three points of the triangle move to the rebound triangle positions while keeping an eye on their respective opponents.

## MAN-TO-MAN DEFENSE

This series illustrates good man-to-man team defense in play situations. Attacking player 12 (in white) has passed the ball to his teammate (23) and has established a set screen in front of him. Note the positions of the defensive players in the black uniforms (11, 12, 13, 15, and 31). Each defensive player is checking his assigned opponent carefully, keeping between him and the basket.

In the second illustration, attacking player 23 is preparing to shoot. Defensive player 13 is floating away from his opponent (24), but he should not turn his back on his opponent and he should be farther back toward the basket.

In the third illustration, attacking player 23 has gotten the shot away and the defensive players have assumed rebound positions. Note the defensive triangle formed by players 11, 13, and 31. Defensive players 12 and 15 are sagging back to the free-throw line to be prepared for a deep rebound.

In the fourth illustration, the defensive-triangle players have successfully blocked their opponents away from the basket and player 13 is making the rebound. Defensive players 12 and 15 are still concentrating on their opponents, but as soon as teammate 13 yells, "Ball," signifying that he has safely secured the ball, they will look for the first outlet pass from 13 and start a fast break.

# ZONE DEFENSES

In the various zone defenses (shown in photos which appear in this chapter), the basic principle is based on playing the ball as opposed to playing an assigned opponent. There are various types of zones: Three-Two (three chasers in the front line of defense with two rebounders in the rear line); Two-Three (two men in the front line and three in the back line); Two-One-Two (two chasers in the front line, one tall rebounder in the center, with two rebounders near the basket); One-Three-One (one chaser in front, three teammates stationed across the court even with the free-throw line, one rebounder under the basket); One-Two-Two (one chaser in front, two teammates near the free-throw line, with two rebounders near the basket).

Although the above zones assign players to the territory surrounding their positions, these territories change with each move of the ball.

## ZONE DEFENSE FORMATIONS

Called the "three-two" zone formation. It was the first zone defense to be developed. The three players in the front line (3, 23, and 12) are known as "chasers." They are constantly on the go and, if they can make an interception, immediately start a fast break for their basket. The two tall players near the basket are rebounders and are expected to get the rebounds and get the ball forward and into the hands of the chasers as quickly as possible.

This is the "two-three" zone and was developed because of the weakness of the three-two zone in the under-basket area. The opponents of the three-two directed their attack toward the under-basket area and outnumbered the two rebounders.

Zone attacks countered the two-three zone by placing a post player in the vicinity of the free-throw line and this led to the development of the two-one-two zone which employs two chasers, a middle man, and two rebounders near the basket.

An easy zone to learn is the one-two-two. Player 23 is the lone chaser when the ball is in the center of the court while teammates 3 and 12 and 22 and 25 form a "box" behind him. When the ball is passed to the side, for example to the attacking team's left, player 3 becomes the chaser and the box is formed by 22 and 23 and 25 and 12.

The one-three-one zone is designed to limit the effectiveness of the tall opponent who operates near the basket. Whenever possible, three men remain in a straight line between the ball and the basket.

# THE MAN-TO-MAN PRESS

This type of defense is applied on a man-to-man basis, with opponents being guarded all over the court. In reality, this was the first defense used in the game of basketball. The defensive players do not retreat to their defensive court. Instead, the opponents are guarded aggressively wherever they are on the court and as soon as they get the ball. The chief objective is to force opponents into making bad passes which will result in interceptions by the pressing players. This defense may be the basic team defense or may be used as a change of pace or when a team is behind and must secure the ball or lose the game.

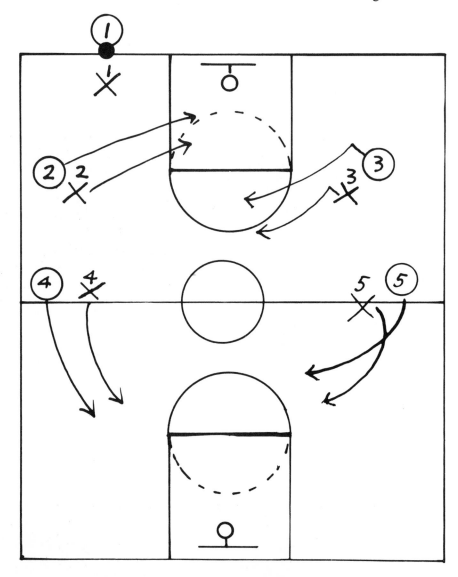

**MAN-TO-MAN PRESS:** Defensive players X1, X2, X3, X4, and X5 are playing their opponents on a straight man-to-man basis and are sticking with them wherever they go.

# THE ZONE PRESS

The zone press operates in much the same manner as the man-to-man press. The difference lies in the fact that the chief emphasis of the zone press lies in territory assignments and playing the ball with the express purpose of trapping an opponent through means of double-teaming. The objectives are the same as in the man-to-man press.

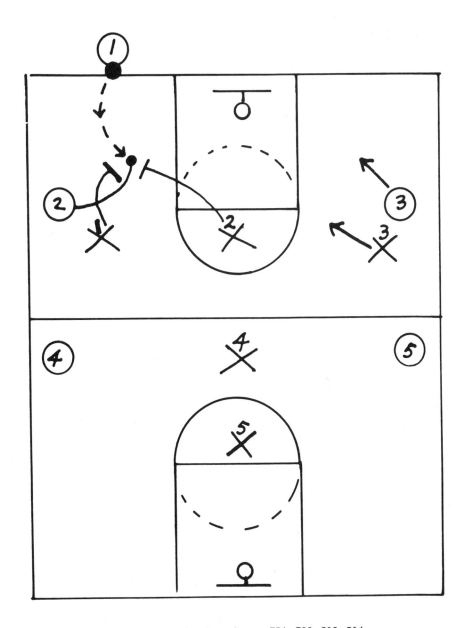

**ZONE PRESS:** Defensive players X1, X2, X3, X4, and X5 are set up in a "Three-One-One" Zone formation and will attempt to trap (double-team) opponents when possible. (Note trap being set by defensive players X1 and X2.)

# CHAPTER VIII

# MAKE THE TEAM

Well, fellows, if you have gotten this far in the book and if you understand what you have read about the basic fundamentals of basketball and the general techniques of team play, it is time for us to go a little further with your preparations to "make the team."

I am sure you realize the importance of "starting right" and the necessity of hard practice, frequent scrimmages, and participation in actual games. And I hope you realize the necessity of broadening your basketball knowledge by reading books and articles about basketball, attending clinics, and going to games with the express purpose of studying great players and observing their special skills and noting what they do on the offense and on the defense.

## SPORTSMANSHIP

A gentleman is a sportsman and vice versa! Good players haven't got time to play dirty, use questionable tactics, contest officials' decisions, commit intentional fouls, gripe about their coach or teammates, think about "getting even" with their opponent, use bad language and fly into a temper, make a show of themselves and end up by getting their teams into trouble. No — good players are too busy *playing* — not *talking* — a good game!

You represent your school, sure. But you represent more than that — you represent your family, your father and mother and brothers and sisters and all your relatives. And remember — your opponent is your guest when you play "at home" and you are his guest when you play "on the road." In either case, a gentleman is at his best when he is the host or a guest.

Shake hands with your opponent when you line up against him for the first time and be *sure* to shake hands with him at the end of the game.

If you lose the game by a big score, tell your opponent and everyone else—"They were too good for us!"

If you lose a close game — "They were better than we were *tonight!*"

If you win by a "runaway" score — "We couldn't do anything wrong tonight!"

If you win a close game — "We were lucky!"

Respect the officials. They know the game and have been trained to officiate. Anyway, good and bad calls even out during a game or a season. Should the call be against you or your team, don't argue. Don't "look daggers." Raise your hand quickly and raise it all the way up. Let your coach take care of the officials. "It's extremely hard to play and officiate at the same time!"

Respect the other team's coach. He's trying his best to win, and so are his players. Make no remarks about his coaching, tactics, or behavior.

## TRAINING

Now we come to training. First, let's make health an objective. And since you want to make the team in basketball, why not condition yourself for the game. If you are too light, put on some weight. How? Well, the doctors tell us we are what we eat. So why not study diet. Eat foods that give your bones and muscles and blood something to work with. Lots of fruit (grapefruit, oranges, prunes, dates, baked apples), vegetables (celery, lettuce, peas, tomatoes and greens, baked or boiled potatoes), meats (roast beef, steak, lamb chops, roast or broiled chicken and turkey, and fresh fish), bread (toast, hard rolls), beverages (milk, one glass with every meal, tomato juice, orange and apple juices, grapefruit juice), eggs (soft boiled, scrambled or poached), cereals (oatmeal, rice, and all modern-day cereals).

Don't overeat and be sure to avoid fried, fatty foods and stuffing yourself — especially before a game.

If you need strength, if your shoulders and arms and legs and hands and fingers need development — well, let's hit some weights and the medicine ball for the big muscles and squeeze handballs and tennis balls for the hands and fingers. Don't forget to make a big hand at every opportunity—stretch your thumb and fingers wide. Rope-climbing is excellent for the upper arms, wrists, fingers, and shoulder muscles.

If you are too slow, practice fast starts, change of pace, change of direction, and short sprints to compensate for natural speed. If you need leg strength and to improve your footwork, jump rope, play handball, hit the weights again with proper exercises to develop the leg muscles. The development of "explosive" power (leaping ability as a combination of jump and reach), rise on your toes with weights on your shoulders and do deep knee bends as an alternate. Nimbleness can be developed through tumbling, rope jumping, shadow boxing and running through tires spaced unevenly on the ground.

## WHAT THE COACH EXPECTS

The most important asset a player can have is love for the game. If a player has this great quality, he can overcome many personal handicaps. The fact that he loves basketball means, in most cases, that he has the right spirit, that he will work hard to succeed, and that he is coachable. A player who is coachable is able to assimilate instructions, is big enough to take criticism, and will keep trying no matter what problems he may be called upon to face.

A coach chooses his squad carefully and he takes many things into consideration—personal traits and emotional qualities as well as playing ability. A candidate's fighting spirit is always high on the list of desirable qualities. A boy with courage and determination will be a help to any team. Naturally, the coach appreciates punctuality and regularity in reporting to practice; this is expected of the boy with the right spirit.

Coaches realize that devotion to practices and games means that a fellow will miss a lot of fun and good times. Practices, games, and devotion to a study program consume about all of a fellow's out-of-school time. Besides, an athlete needs lots of sleep and rest. But there are a lot of rewards which compensate for the sacrifices — good health, pride of accomplishment, belonging to a team, recognition as an athlete, respect of family, friends, the community, and your schoolmates.

All coaches appreciate perseverance. A boy who sticks to the instruction directions of the coach and works hard at improving his game is bound to attract the attention and interest of the coach. Right here, it is important that you understand that criticism by the coach means he is *interested* in you. Some fellows just can't take criticism and they are handicapped at the very beginning. The youngster who keeps in mind that constructive criticism is the job of the coach will make giant strides in developing his abilities.

Coaches place a high premium on the "desire to win!" Although the basic responsibility of a coach is to teach the game of basketball to his players, he is always looking for the fellow who plays the game to the hilt; the youngster who fights with all his heart for his school, his teammates, and the game. One of our most respected attorney generals once said: "A game worth playing is a game worth winning!"

Consistency is a virtue, a most important part of any game or vocation. The coach prefers to "go" with the consistent player when he has a choice. He likes the steady boy who delivers "up to par" all the time. The flash in the pan, the do-or-die player is all right for a crisis — provided he is "up" when the crisis arrives. Selecting the player who is sometimes hot and sometimes cold (inconsistent) is a shot in the dark, a poor substitute for the player who may not be brilliant but who is steady and dependable and above all — consistent. "What coach could ever complain about a player who gives *all he has all the time?*"

## BE A REAL ATHLETE

First — dress, look, and act like an athlete. Choose "real" athletes as your example and be a "real" athlete for the many youngsters who will look up to you as their hero. And dream your dreams unafraid — all real athletes have done the same thing. All the great ones had dreams of making the team; winning the big game; making all-city, all-county, all-state, and ALL-AMERICA. They had their dreams the same as you have yours — and they did something about them.

A real athlete knows that he's going somewhere. He's determined to be a success. He's up in his studies and in his eligibility, and he has spirit, hustle, and loyalty. He boosts his team, his school, his coach, his teammates, and his fellow students. He has emotional control. He's not a show-off and he's a man all the way. Good enough to make the team and big enough to do what's right — on his own.

The real athlete never "chickens out" on anything — if it's right and decent. The real athlete has enough guts to say "Count me out" when it comes to breaking training and destroying property. No, the real athlete doesn't

have to demonstrate his independence or individuality by getting out of line.

Fun? Sure! A happy team is a winning team. But there's a limit, a point where fun can become obnoxious and lead to trouble. The real athlete knows when to stop. And he's got the guts to do it. When it comes to a showdown, the fellow who *believes* in the right thing and who has the guts to *do* the right thing will turn out to be the leader, whether he is a sub, the manager, or the water boy.

## CONDUCT ON TRIPS

So you've made the grade and you're on your first trip as a member of a team. The pressure is really on you now, fellow. Yep, you're traveling "on the road" as the representative of everything your school and your community stand for. That means you're somebody — and you have to act like a "somebody." You have to make sure your clothes are clean and pressed and that you have a neat hair cut and that your hands and face and body are clean. You're courteous on the bus, on the train, in the hotel, on the streets, in the opponent's school and on the playing court. You're somebody — you have a responsibility to all the people who put you where you are, and that's a lot of representing. How big *are* you?

## PRACTICE TIPS

Basketball is a year-round game. An old saying goes something like this: "You learn to skate in the summer and to swim in the winter." That was before the days of the year-around ice-skating rink and indoor swimming pools, but it had nothing to do with seasons. No, it was concerned with the mind — the ability to *think* basketball in the spring and in the summer and in the fall and to practice mentally in any season.

When you practice physically — hustle! Produce during every second you are on the court. Hustle in the drills and in the scrimmages. And, if you are tired and must relax or rest, do it when your team has the ball. Never let down when you are playing on the defense.

Practice just as hard in the team workouts as you play in a game. Hit the floor if you have to do so to get the ball — go all out; remember, you play like you practice. Work at full speed *all* the time. A champion works hard and plays hard — in the practices and in the games.

## PRE-GAME WARM-UP

Take your time warming-up and concentrate on your position skills. Start slow and gradually speed up your moves until you are "loose" and ready for fast action. Then, and only then, open up and concentrate on your game speed; give your passes and dribbling and shooting all you've got.

In your shooting drills, start close to the basket and work back to your maximum range, keeping in mind that you are trying to familiarize yourself with the floor and the lights and the crowd and the basket under game conditions. Game conditions and practice conditions differ greatly. Don't fool around — work! Get the feel of the floor, move to your favorite shooting and position area. Get acquainted with the shadows and the crowd movements and the "spots" from which you know you can hit.

Be sure to take your free-throws. This is where the close game will be won. Use your free and easy movements and the same techniques you have practiced. Concentrate and make every shot count. Every shot is for the championship. "You shoot in the games like you shoot when you practice."

Don't look for a friend or a fan in the crowd or act nonchalant. This is for keeps! You won't be looking around during the game. Why look around now? Be all business and concentrate on what you're doing.

## GAME PLAY

Now we're getting down to applied basketball — to the game. *Every* player must possess certain skills and qualities. Every player must be able to do something without the ball, know how to screen, cut, feed teammates.

Hustle on the court, off the court, and on the bench. That's right — on the bench. How can you hustle on the bench? Easy. Be in every play, cheer your teammates all the way. If you're on the bench, you're on the team!

On the offense, keep the ball moving and don't force your passes. When you have the ball, be ready to pass to a teammate if he maneuvers his opponent out of position and cuts for the basket. When you don't have the ball — do something. Move!

Give defensive play all you've got. Run backwards and point out your opponent when retreating to your defensive court. Don't be lazy, turn your back and trot back on defense. Your opponent is likely to "run up your back." Face up to your opponents and point out your man and "talk it up."

When you are matched up with an opponent, be the boss. Dog him every move he makes — be his shadow. "No one appreciates good defensive play?" Only your teammates and the coach and the real basketball fans and your opponents and the coach of the other team — to list a few. Oh, yes, add yourself to the list — your self-respect.

Don't play to the crowd! Concentrate on the game and your teammates. Know the score — the time left to play, the number of fouls checked up against you, the number of fouls your opponent has drawn, the number of time-outs left in the game, and "feel" the trend of the game. If your team is ahead and the opponents are coming fast, slow down your team's moves, break the opponent's tempo. If you are behind and are moving up fast on the opponents, keep the drive going! Talk and hustle and take care of your personal defensive responsibilities first and then try to help your teammates. Remember, the good dribbler likes to have his opponent lunge and try to take the ball away from him. Don't be a sucker. Forget the ball! Concentrate on the dribbler and force him away from his objective. If your opponent is extremely fast and likes to cut and drive, give him room. If he is a dead shot, keep a hand up all the time to discourage his shots and keep him busy; if you can keep the ball away from him, you've got him in your pocket.

Offensive play is fun and defensive play is hard work! That's right. But why be *half* a player?

## POSITION PLAY

BACK COURT PLAYERS — OFFENSE

Back court players are "take-charge" guys; the quarterbacks; the guys who protect the ball and bring it safely up court; who set up the plays and reflect the team's confidence and aggressiveness. They're the sparkplugs, the coaches on the court. They are alert, confident, aggressive, determined, steady and dependable. As *they* go — so goes the team!

*Offensive responsibilities in the back court*

Lead the fast break. Get the ball up court before the opponents can set up their defense. Go all the way or stop at the free-throw line and shoot (if uncovered) or get the ball to the uncovered player. Hold up the play if the "quick" score seems doubtful. Hold up the ball and wait for the "set" offense to form.

Protect the ball on the slow advance (cross and force the opponents to move laterally in covering the ball).

Be prepared to meet any form of the press (man-to-man or zone — full court or half court).

Be alert to the possibility of initiating your team's offense following a deep rebound, interception, fumble by opponents, after an outlet pass, or from a held-ball situation.

*Offensive responsibilities in the front court* (back court players)

Always anticipate the quick score (look for loose teammate).

Complete fast break responsibilities.

Form the set offense and initiate the plays.

Use give-and-go techniques with back court teammate or teammates and corner men.

Feed the post player, the pivot man, and corner teammates.

Make sure of "defensive balance."

Point up (keep in line with the ball) to enable teammates to return the ball safely to you if a play is unsuccessful.

Possess a good "outside" set shot, jumper, drive and lay-in shot, and the stop-set (one- or two-hand).

Know how to cut off the post or pivot player for plays.

Employ all types of set and moving screens.

Help establish "double" screens (usually by aligning beside a front court teammate in a "set" position).

Understand clear-out techniques (passing the ball to a teammate, cutting behind him, receiving the ball back and hitting the teammate when he cuts away).

Know how to use the freeze and how to set it up and when and how to use a "possession" offense.

Maneuver for the "one shot" play when a period is ending or the clock is running out.

Know assignments in out-of-bounds plays.

Be expert in one-on-one plays (teammates cut away clear one side of court so a player with the ball may attempt to outmaneuver his opponent and get off a shot, dribble in for the lay-in, or draw a foul).

*Important passes for back court players*

Two-hand overhead (makes a big man out of a little man), bounce pass, hook, chest or "snap" pass, tap give-and-go pass, over- and under-arm passes for fast-break use.

DEFENSIVE RESPONSIBILITIES

Set up the defensive formation. Usually the first man back on defense. Talk. Point. Hustle. Assemble teammates.

Harass opposing back court players.

Sag and float to help defend under-basket area weakness or to stop opponent's big man.

Deep position for rebounds.

THE BIG MAN (POST OR PIVOT PLAYER)

*Must possess scoring shots. Post Position* (usually in outer half of free-throw circle): One-hand set, one-hand jumper, dribble and lay-in, dribble-stop shots. *Pivot Position* (near basket): Turn shot, pivot shot, step-away hook, jump spin, one-hand set, straight jumper, one-hand push (with and without fake).

*Passing* (master of rebound long and outlet passes). *Post Position:* Under-arm passes, hook, bounce and back flips and bounces, cross face and body, quarterback hand-offs. *Pivot Position:* Hand signals to designate where he wants the ball passed. Same passes as post player plus more feints and fakes as preliminary moves to own shots.

### Maneuvering

Must know how to maneuver in both positions to frustrate attempts of opponent to play him in front or on the side (turns, spins, cut away and return, etc.).

Master of fishhook to help back court teammates who are pressed while bringing ball up court.

Ability to dribble out of trouble following a rebound or when pressed.

### Offensive Rebounding

Get ball and pass out.

Get ball and go back up for shot.

Tap back (high rebounds he cannot catch).

Tap-in for a score.

## BIG MAN DEFENSE

Plays opponent in front when he is in scoring territory.

Keeps his opponent from securing favorite scoring position by getting there first.

Switching ability (must call out the switches).

Block shots of opponents who break free from teammates

Use "umbrella" defense (arms and hands spread high over head of opponent who cuts under basket with the ball).

## CORNER PLAYER (FORWARD)

### Offense — Back court

Able to bring ball up court when necessary.

Make outlet passes following rebounds.

Fill outside lanes or assume middle lane responsibilities on fast break.

Assist in advancing ball from back court to front court.

Fishhook back to help back court teammates when they are pressed.

Know how to oppose full-court or semi-press (man-to-man or zone).

### Offense — Front court

Handle ball for plays near sidelines.

Work plays with back court teammates and expert in use of give-and-go.

Feed post and pivot big man and work plays with him.

Expert in corner and sideline clear-out moves and plays.

Master all passes used by back court teammates and the big man.

### Shots

Corner one- and two-hand sets, corner jumper, drive and jumper, drive and lay-up or lay-in.

### Moves

One-on-one, base line drive, change of direction, change of pace, and cuts off of big man.

### Defense

Back court player's defensive duties: front, slide, switch, never lose opponents, delay fast break plays near basket, play big man defensive position in emergency, rebound techniques, boxing-out ability.

## INDIGENOUS... INDIVIDUAL OFFENSE TIPS

### BODY BALANCE

The offensive player should assume the "boxer's" posture and stance and use his arms and hands as balance regulators. He should be sure his weight is distributed evenly on the balls of the feet.

### FOOTWORK

Basketball is a game of motion and a player moves on his feet. Good footwork, therefore, is a "must." Footwork covers starts, stops, change of direction, pivots, "angling" away, cutting, screening, driving, the offensive roll, and jumping.

### Fast Starts

A quick start requires short steps. Drop your shoulders forward and push hard with the rear foot. Thrust your arms and shoulders forward and "go!"

### Hard Stops

The fast stop follows one or two hard, short strides with the knees bent and the center of gravity (tail) carried low. The feet slap down hard on the floor and the toes should point slightly outward.

### Change of Direction

This starts with the "stop" principles discussed above. The "one-two" count should be used with the front foot slapping down hard on the "one" count and the rear foot following on through to jab into the floor on the "two" count. Now, with the body lowered as in the stop, pres-

sure is applied through the front foot to drive the shoulders in the opposite direction. A crossover in the same direction with the forward foot precedes the short steps which lead to a fast start.

### Pivots

Turns and pivots utilize stop techniques and the "one-two" count. If cutting or dribbling to the right and a pivot to the left is desired, the left foot would stop on the "one" count. The right foot would follow on through and become the forward foot on the "two" count. Now, the forward foot (right) is swung back and to the right. This forces the body to spin to the rear on the left foot (pivot foot) ending up in a quarter, half, three quarter, or full pivot.

### Angling Away

A player "angles" away when he cuts *away* from the ball. This angling draws his opponent away from the teammate with the ball and also enables the cutter to set screens for teammates who may cut toward the ball or the basket.

### Cutting

This term applies to hard cutting (running) for the basket. However, timing the cut is important and the cutter should not drive for the basket unless a teammate is in good position to pass the ball to him.

### Screening

This ability is the mark of a good team player. Screens may be inside (between a teammate and his opponent) or outside (behind a teammate's opponent). They may also be made to the side, to the back, and they may be set or moving and with or without the ball. Develop screening ability so you face the basket during and after the screen.

### Driving

This move generally is concerned with the man with the ball. He dribbles hard for the basket with the shoulder next to his opponent carried close to the floor (lowered). He dribbles with the opposite hand and tries to use low, control bounces of the ball. Good drivers usually score close to the basket (the sure shoot) and draw many fouls.

### Offensive Roll

This maneuver resembles the "defensive" roll and is a must to avoid charging an opponent when moving toward a teammate.

### Jumping

Leaping for a tap or a rebound starts with a crouch. An explosive upward thrust with feet, ankles, knees, trunk, shoulders and arms (all coordinated) helps gain extra height. Many inches can be added to your leap through regular practice on the upward thrust. (The intelligent use of weight-lifting exercises can increase your leap as much as eight or ten inches.)

**TWO-MAN OFFENSIVE PLAY:** ("Turn-Around").

This series illustrates several good offensive principles. In the first picture, offensive player 15 has used a "shot" pass to feed the ball to teammate 31 (pivot player). The pivot man came in high and caught the ball at the top of his leap. Note that the pivot man's legs are wide spread (rebound fashion).

In the second picture, the pivot man has landed on the court and, still holding the ball above his head, is in the process of pivoting to face the basket. The backcourt player (15) is shown maneuvering his defensive opponent (23) into the "pick" or a position which will force a defensive switch in which opponent 25 will cover the offensive cutter 15 and defensive player 23 will attempt to guard opponent 31. If defensive player 25 switches to cover opponent 15, the pivot man (31) can shoot unrestricted (set or jumper) or dribble in for a layup shot. If defensive player 25 does not switch, the pivot man can pass the ball to teammate 15 for an unrestricted shot.

# DECEPTION

## Faking

Fakes are made with the ball and with the feet. The idea is to lure your opponent into shifting his weight in the direction opposite that in which you wish to move.

## Feinting

This trickery is performed with the head, eyes and/or the body — turning the head, shifting the eyes, or moving the shoulders and turning in the direction opposite that in which you intend to go.

## Vision

Looking straight ahead but "seeing" to the right and to the left as well, is called peripheral or marginal vision. Work on it and when you are the playmaker or have the ball, wear a "dead-pan" expression to conceal your intentions. It works!

## "Dummy"

Playing "dummy" is fun. You pretend to be interested in something far removed from basketball by looking away from the ball or the action and using peripheral vision to see "everything." You also delay your move as long as possible to further lull your opponent into confident security. Then, you move like lightning — to the ball or to the basket!

# PASSING

## Control

Keep both hands on the ball as long as possible and fake your passes before you release the ball. And — use fingertip control.

# DRIBBLING

## The Touch

It's a fingertip game! Educate your fingers so they manipulate the ball as though it was on the end of a rubber band.

**FAKING:** The importance of good offensive faking is shown above. In the first picture, offensive player 12 (dark shirt) faked a shot and then feinted a dribble to his left (13's right). Defensive player 13 fell for the maneuver and advanced his right foot in the direction of the feint.

As shown in the second picture, defensive player 13 is now in a poor guarding position. Offensive player 12 can dribble around his opponent or make an unrestricted pass (push or bounce) to his right.

## SHOOTING

### The Nine Steps

1. Grasp the ball with the fingertips. Spread the fingers. Make a big hand! Hold the ball loosely.

2. Balance the body — feet separated slightly, knees and body flexed.

3. Concentrate the eyes on the target (rim or backboard).

4. "See" the shot. Visualize the path the ball will take and the force necessary to cover the arc and the distance.

5. Use the "elbow squeeze." Pinch the elbows together before the shot begins and while aiming the ball (one- or two-hand shot).

6. Aim — jiggle — unlock wrists.

7. Start the shot. Start from the toes and the balls of the feet. The power is generated up through the ankles and lower legs, the thighs, trunk, shoulders, arms, wrists and out to the fingertips.

8. Release the ball from the ends of the fingertips.

9. Follow through with the flow or force *after* the ball is released.

**UNLOCKING THE WRISTS:** The good basketball player keeps two hands on the ball as long as possible. Maintaining possession enables a player to control the ball. For example, if a player attempts to pass the ball with one hand, he may not be able to stop it if an opponent should anticipate the pass and start for an interception. The same is true should a teammate fail to realize a pass is going to be attempted. With two hands in control, the passer can hang on to the ball (almost to the last split-second) and stop the pass. Further, two-hand possession enables the player to start a dribble or go for a shot as well as fake or feint with the ball.

The series illustrates "unlocking" the wrists. This unlocking is present in one- or two-hand passes, shots and in starting a dribble. It consists of dropping hands (ball) downward from the wrists and toward the floor; bringing the hands quickly back to the original position and then releasing the ball from the fingertips (the palms are never in contact with the ball in playing basketball). Some players unlock their wrists so swiftly that the eye cannot catch the action.

**DEVELOP "SNAP":** Sitting on a chair and attempting shots at the basket is a fine way to develop elbow, wrist and fingertip "snap." Force yourself to propel the ball with the elbow (elbows), wrist (wrists) and fingertips *only* in shooting the one- or two-hand shots. (Shots must be *clean* — the ball touches nothing but the net as it swishes through.)

After you have mastered the shot from the chair, go a step further and try for goals while sitting on the floor. Here, you may be forced to use an upward thrust of your legs and back.

# CHAPTER X

# SPECIAL PLAYER TIPS

## DEFENSE

## INDIVIDUAL DEFENSE TIPS

### BODY BALANCE

The defensive player should use the "wrestler's" posture and stance. Keep your weight distributed evenly on the balls of the feet and be prepared to stick with your opponent "without crossing the feet." One hand should be advanced toward the opponent and the other should be carried at the side (extended).

### STANCE

One foot should be slightly advanced and the other placed to the rear. They should be slightly staggered to the width of the shoulders.

### FLOOR POSITION

The "in-line" principle has been discussed. Coaches permit many variations of this principle, but be sure you do *not* "turn your head" to see the ball or the action.

### FOOTWORK

Use of the wrestler's stance and the glide (one foot following the other without crossing) should enable you to keep between your opponent and the basket. If a hard-cutting opponent gets the jump on you it may be necessary to use a long backward step or even turn sideways and run to keep up with him.

### FRONT — SLIDE — SWITCH

These moves are the "guts" of defensive play (man-to-man defense). You must master them (see page 94) and those which follow in order to be a good defensive player.

### FIGHT THROUGH SCREENS

When opposed by an opponent's screen — (moving or set) — don't stop! Fight through until you catch up with your opponent unless a teammate calls for a switch.

### OVER THE TOP

When an opponent gives you room in cutting around a teammate, try to go with him (over the top). Never go behind a teammate in trying to keep up with your opponent. This error gives your opponent an unguarded shot at the basket.

### GUARDING A SCORER

Play him tightly if he has the ball (point of the ball). If he is too fast for you, give him some room but keep your extended hand moving in his face. Overshifting may help when he goes one direction more often than the other. Above all, concentrate!

### GUARDING A CUTTER

Give him room when he is at a distance from the basket. Know where the ball is and anticipate his moves. A long back step is important when he cuts but make sure he doesn't change direction on you.

### GUARDING THE DRIBBLER

If your opponent can't dribble the ball "both ways" overshift to his strength. Keep your body low and your weight back. Try to discourage his moves by keeping your hands low and try to force him to dribble to the sidelines. Stabbing for the ball draws you out of position and a good dribbler will leave you "at the post!"

**STANCE:** Henry "Hank" Luisetti, Stanford University, was three times All-America and one of the first of the great one-handed shooters. Hank was such a wonderful offensive player that few experts recognized his defensive ability. Study this photograph and not the focusing of the eyes (defensive players should concentrate on opponents' "belt buckles" since most offensive players employ eye feints).

The positions of the hands and feet and the low center of gravity mean Hank is ready to move quickly in any direction. Luisetti's weight is back and with his right foot ready for use as a pivot foot, he can swing his left foot back and use the boxer's shuffle to go with his opponent to the right (Hank's left). Should the opponent cut or dribble to Hank's left, Luisetti is already in position to use the boxer's glide to go with him.

### GUARDING THE PLAYMAKER

Play him closely. Playing the ball "tight" not only disturbs the playmaker but disrupts his team's offense as well. An expert defensive player will try to guard the playmaker so well that his teammates have difficulty getting the ball to him.

### GUARDING THE MAN WITHOUT THE BALL

The distance your opponent is away from the basket determines how closely he should be played. Tighten up as he approaches the basket and be prepared for a change of direction. Try to keep between him and the ball without getting so far out of position that you cannot recover should he make a sudden move.

### GUARDING THE BIG MAN

This is a tough assignment. Most defensive players guard big men from the front when they are within twelve feet of the basket. Moving from side to side with the passing of the ball is effective and may discourage passes to the big man. Keep your hands moving and don't fall for the big man's fakes and feints when he gets the ball.

### BOXING-OUT

Every player should be able to box-out his opponent. Most players fail to execute this important defensive maneuver because they turn their heads to watch the ball instead of concentrating on their opponents. "Don't be a head-turner!"

### REBOUNDING

Not all the rebounds are made by the big fellows. All players are expected to be alert and to make rebounds. Height is not the determining factor in getting the ball. Getting into position and then "timing" the leap is vital. Get into position, shift with your opponent to block him out, time your leap so you will get the rebound at the extreme height of your leap — and get the ball into play as quickly as possible.

### BLOCKING SHOTS

The "stop" results when a defensive player times his opponent's shot perfectly. The defensive player waits for the precise moment when his opponent shoots and then gets a hand on the ball or knocks it away from the target.

The "save" is the play which you often see

when the man with the ball is far ahead of a defensive player and on his way for an easy score. Then, from nowhere, it seems, a defensive player appears in time to bat the ball away from the goal (usually after it is in the air).

### DOUBLE TEAMING

All defensive players should be alert to double-team possibilities. When an opponent is in a poor passing position or has turned his back on his teammates, the opportunity for double-teaming is present. Try to prevent the opponent from passing the ball (tie him up).

### INTERCEPTIONS

Play "dummy" and try for interceptions whenever you think you have a good chance to get the ball. Don't take chances, though. Concentrate first on defensing your immediate opponent.

### TALKING

Talking to teammates is a vital part of any defense. The player who is closest to the basket is charged with the responsibility of advising teammates when they are in danger of "picks" and it is his job to call the "switch" when a pick is obvious. He should also say, "stay" when there is no danger of a pick and call "Heads up!" when it looks like a pick may be attempted.

**THE FOLLY OF "TURNING THE HEAD"** to watch the ball or an opponent is illustrated in this series. In picture one, offensive player 15 passes the ball to teammate 12. Defensive player 23 has turned his head to watch the ball.

In picture two, offensive player 15 has taken advantage of the "head turning" error by defensive player 23 and has cut away from the ball and toward the basket. (Note that offensive player 12 is faking a shot to bring opponent 12's hand up.) This will enable offensive player 12 an opening for a bounce pass to the cutter (15).

In the third photograph, the disaster which has overtaken defensive player 23 is clearly shown. His opponent (15) has broken free, gathered up the ball (bounce pass) and now will have an unguarded shot at the basket. (Don't turn your head. If you *must* watch the ball or an opponent other than your own, drop back and away from your opponent so you can see him as well as the ball *without* turning the head.)

**GOOD GUARDING TECHNIQUES** by all five defensive players (black uniforms) are shown in this photograph, with one possible exception. The exception is the defensive player guarding the man with the ball. He could (depending on his opponent) guard him more closely and aggressively. However, the center of the court is wide open and if the man with the ball is an expert at "one-on-one" play, it might be dangerous.

Note the defensive positions of the players in dark uniforms. All have good body positions; one hand up with the other extended to the side; and are concentrating on their respective opponents (without turning their heads) even though some are using "pressure" defensive positions (playing between personal opponents and the ball).

**"CONTROL OF THE BOARDS MEANS VICTORY!"** is a well known basketball axiom. This photograph shows the all-important "rebound-triangle." Note that the defensive players have formed a triangle under the basket with A in front of the basket and in the center of the 3-second lane and with B and C on each side of the lane and close to the backboard. This triangle formation blocks opponents out of the three most vulnerable paths to the basket. Learn to get into the vacant angle of the triangle! Then, box out the opponent who tries to get past you and gain the "inside" position for the rebound.

**THE FREE-THROW FORMATION** usually assumed by offensive and defensive teams. Naturally, the game conditions determine whether or not they will be varied to use a press (shooting team) or freeze (defensive team). Note the positions of the players "on the lane." The player guarding the shooter (23) will step into the lane and box the shooter away from the ball as soon as it hits the ring or the backboard.

This picture is probably as good as any with which to end your book. It exemplifies the importance of a large blackboard in teaching and coaching. The blackboard can be used time and again to stress important training and playing hints as well as draw out (diagram) important offensive and defensive moves.

On the right, a series of individual points have been listed to remind shooters of the principles behind expert marksmanship. On the left, two phases of team play are diagrammed. The defensive team (X players) are in a "One-Three-One" Zone defense (originated by the writer). Check the slides and moves made by X1, X2, X3, X4 and X5 in following the ball. Keep in mind that teams using a zone defense, play the ball first and the oppo-

nents second. In other words, they shift with the ball and try to defend the area in which the player and/or players in possession are situated. Note that there are always three players between the ball and the basket.

Offensively, players A, B, C, D and E are set up (starting positions) in a "One-Three-One" Attack. This formation changes as soon as the ball is passed to either side of the court. Although not much offensive action is shown, it is important to keep in mind that fast movement of the ball and players is important in securing good shots at the basket.

The zone defense is used extensively in high school and college basketball but has been "outlawed" in professional basketball (to speed up the action and satisfy spectator interest).

Well, fellows, that's it!

Remember — "Winners never quit — Quitters never win!

But

Worse than a quitter — one who won't try . . .